SOE in Czechoslovakia

The Special Operations Executive's
Czech Section in WW2

An Official History

FRONTLINE BOOKS

SOE IN CZECHOSLOVAKIA
The Special Operations Executive's Czech Section in WW2

This edition published in 2022 by Frontline Books,
an imprint of Pen & Sword Books Ltd,
47 Church Street, Barnsley, S. Yorkshire, S70 2AS

This book is based on file reference HS 7/108, from a series of SOE records held at The National Archives, Kew, and is licensed under the Open Government Licence v3.0. Appendix H is taken from AIR 20/8459, Second Draft, at The National Archives, Kew and licensed under the Open Government Licence v3.0.

Text alterations and additions © Frontline Books

ISBN: 978 1 39908 275 4

All rights reserved. No part of this publication may be reproduced, stored in or introduced into a retrieval system, or transmitted, in any form, or by any means (electronic, mechanical, photocopying, recording or otherwise) without the prior written permission of the publisher. Any person who does any unauthorized act in relation to this publication may be liable to criminal prosecution and civil claims for damages. CIP data records for this title are available from the British Library.

Typeset by Mac Style
Printed and bound in the UK by CPI Group (UK) Ltd,
Croydon, CR0 4YY.

Pen & Sword Books Limited incorporates the imprints of Atlas, Archaeology, Aviation, Discovery, Family History, Fiction, History, Maritime, Military, Military Classics, Politics, Select, Transport, True Crime, Air World, Frontline Publishing, Leo Cooper, Remember When, Seaforth Publishing, The Praetorian Press, Wharncliffe Local History, Wharncliffe Transport, Wharncliffe True Crime and White Owl.

For a complete list of Pen & Sword titles please contact

PEN & SWORD BOOKS LIMITED
47 Church Street, Barnsley, South Yorkshire, S70 2AS, England
E-mail: enquiries@pen-and-sword.co.uk
Website: www.pen-and-sword.co.uk

Or

PEN AND SWORD BOOKS
1950 Lawrence Rd, Havertown, PA 19083, USA
E-mail: Uspen-and-sword@casematepublishers.com
Website: www.penandswordbooks.com

Contents

Publisher's Note   viii
Introduction   ix

Chapter 1	Pre-Hostilities Clandestine Activities	1
Chapter 2	Early 1940 and First S.O.E. Contacts	2
Chapter 3	Problems and Achievements	6
Chapter 4	The Czech Departments	9
Chapter 5	Activities in the Field	12
Chapter 6	The 1942-1943 Season	13
	The C.O.S. Directive	13
	Occupational Scheme	14
	The Operational Season 1943-1944	15
Chapter 7	Operations from the Mediterranean Theatre	16
	Transfer of Operations from U.K. to the Mediterranean	17
	Sorties from North Africa	18
	Provision of Airlift, Italy	18
	Operations 1944	19
	Slovak Rising	20
	"Windproof"	22
	"Mica"	25
	"Silica" – Czech Troops in Northern Italy	26
	Summary of Operations in 1944	27

	Operations in 1945	27
	Protectorate Rising	29
	Summary of Operations in 1945	33
	Summary of Czech Operations From Italy	33
	Structure of the Czech Section	34
	Move of H.Q. S.O.M. to Siena	35
	Effect of Move to Siena on Czech Operations	35
	Changeover to American Airforce	36
	Liaison with O.S.S	36
	Liaison with I.S.L.D.	37
	Liaison with P.W.B.	37
	Liaison with "A" Force (I.S.9)	37
	Liaison with Air Forces	38
Chapter 8	"Wolfram"	39
Chapter 9	Operation *Bauxite*	43
Chapter 10	"Manganese"	48
Chapter 11	"Sulphur"	57
Chapter 12	"Chalk"	59
Chapter 13	"Glucinium"	61
Chapter 14	"Clay"	70
Chapter 15	"Carbon"	80
Chapter 16	"Tungsten" (S.I.S.)	86
Chapter 17	"Platinum"	93
Chapter 18	Conclusion	107

Appendices

Appendix A	Situation of S.O.E. Parties in the Field, 4 January 1945	111
Appendix B	Czechoslovak S.O.E. Parties Summary	114
Appendix C	Summary of Operations	115
Appendix D	Stores Expended on Czech Operations in 1944	122
Appendix E	Stores Expended on Czech Operations in 1945	125
Appendix F	The Slovak Rising	130
Appendix G	The Prague Rising	136
Appendix H	RAF and SOE: Central Europe, Supplied by Aircraft Based in the UK and Mediterranean	141

Publisher's Note

This 'official history' was originally compiled by Mr. F.E. Keary, Major P.W. Auster and Major G.I. Klauber at around the end of the Second World War. The main text and its various appendices are reproduced here as close to their original form as possible. Aside from correcting obvious spelling mistakes or typographical errors, we have strived to keep the edits and alterations to the absolute minimum.

Introduction

From an S.O.E. point of view, Czechoslovakia differed in one or two respects from the other European countries. In the first place, it had been under full German occupation since early 1939. In the second place, the whole country was honeycombed with German enclaves and colonies, most of whom had been won to the Nazi cause, and many of whom were in positions of commercial or industrial influence, or at least well in the way of keeping constant observation on all important Czechoslovak activities. Numbers of these Germans spoke Czech and mixed with the Czechs.

During the first year, the occupation authorities took full control of many of the larger Protectorate concerns, whether financial, commercial or industrial.

As a whole, the Czechs, by race, history and inclination, are particularly hostile to the Germans. President Beneš had, therefore, seen to it before leaving his country at the end of 1938 that underground organisations were established.

A peculiarity of the country lay in its being completely landlocked. Slovakia had to all appearance voluntarily placed itself under German influence in March 1939 in exchange for freedom from what were imagined to be Czech shackles. S.O.E. was little concerned with this Eastern Province until later in the war. A German-controlled demarcation wall, however porous, stood between Slovakia and Moravia; conditions in the east were unknown to S.O.E., and initially they were concerned only with Bohemia-Moravia as a completely beleaguered operational area. Indeed, in only one case was any attempt made by S.O.E., or as far as is known by "C", to infiltrate any agent overland: this took place from Istanbul, and the man's journey to

Bratislava from the time of leaving England lasted some eighteen months. The frequency or value of the Czech D.M.I.'s overland routes used by a few commercial representatives between the Protectorate and Stockholm or elsewhere were never ascertained to S.O.E. satisfaction.

At the opening of hostilities in September 1939 no prospects of Russian hostilities against Germany could be foreseen, so at first there was little thought of working towards pre-invasion plans for the Protectorate. The initial task before S.O.E. was that of causing the maximum hindrance and damage to the German war effort in respect of the Protectorate as a military concentration area, training ground, and focal transport area. The establishment of communications was the first requirement.

The second factor in S.O.E. plans was the disruption of German economic resources. Whilst the production of Czech steel and heavy industries hardly exceed 10% of the Reich output, the same being roughly true of coal and armaments, there were considerable potentialities as a safe area to which German factories might be displaced out of range of air attack. Bohemia and Moravia later became great forward depots alongside Poland for the supplying of the Eastern Front.

Another considerable economic potentiality lay in the skill of Czech artisans and industrial workers; indeed, in the case of the Czechs the Germans were much less concerned with transferring slave labour or with recruiting militia than elsewhere. The German aim was to win a more or less contented nation to their side, to have them work in their home industries, emphatically including agriculture, and where desirable to reinforce the skilled working resources of Reich industry by their aid.

Mr. F.E. Keary, Major P.W. Auster and Major G.I. Klauber

Chapter 1

Pre-Hostilities Clandestine Activities

The underground organisation initiated by President Beneš was divided originally into a military and a civilian wing, most probably each with its own courier and communications network.

On the British side, "C" partially aided and abetted Czech patriotic effort. S.O.E. was not concerned.

During the whole of 1939 subsequent to the occupation on 15 Mar there was a small but clandestine flow of Czech Service Officers and also inventors and industrial workers with armaments designs outwards through Poland and Hungary as well as by other routes. It is interesting to note that the Czechs took the very deliberate step of transferring their D.M.I. and other important persons direct to Great Britain rather than to Paris or even to Moscow as no doubt they were invited to do.

Here, nevertheless, a word should be said about the Czech attitude towards those, and particularly S.O.E., who called upon them to undertake risks at home in the Allied cause. The prevalent Slav reserve and suspicion were greatly deepened both by Munich itself and by our comparative timidity or inability to undertake clandestine measures on a larger scale between the occupation and the outbreak of hostilities.

The Czechs for example would have liked to see numbers of technical troops and airmen transferred for service in Britain. They felt at the time that they were discouraged by us in such projects.

Chapter 2

Early 1940 and First S.O.E. Contacts

Moving from the pre-hostilities period to early 1940, the Czechs have told us that at the same time as the well-known German reprisals against Czech students in Prague in Oct 1939 more far-reaching action was taken against the entire underground movement. Certain losses were sustained and in the New Year of 1940 the civil and military wings of the underground system were coalesced and probably this was accompanied by a substantial reduction in internal courier lines and other means of communication.

General, then Colonel, Gubbins, under whom Major P.A. Wilkinson was already serving, first met Colonel (now General) Moravec in Paris in February 1940. Colonel Gubbins' real appointment was Leader of the Polish Mission. In regard to the Czechs, the Colonel was acting as M.I.R.'s agent or liaison officer. Besides Moravec, General Ingr and General Miroslav (then Czech C-in-C in France) also took part in short discussion. President Beneš was almost certainly closely informed of these very general talks.

After April 1940, Colonel Gubbins and also Major Wilkinson proceeded on other duties.

On 18 Nov 40 Brigadier Gubbins, aided after December by Major Wilkinson, took over the immediate direction of Czech matters for S.O.E. Collaboration was developed with Colonel Moravec's staff. Lieut-Colonel Tichy was the Czechoslovak Liaison Officer with the S.O.E; Major Fryc was shortly afterwards associated with him: Major Strankmuller was throughout Colonel Moravec's Assistant.

The Czechoslovak Authorities in Great Britain as elsewhere in the world had already been absent from their own country for the best part of a year. It may be assumed that acting under President Beneš' orders, Moravec's principal consideration was the re-establishment of communications with the home country.

However much the Czech nation and even its leaders abroad were satisfied at heart to lie low during the German occupation and wait patiently for the passing of temporary hostile domination, doubtless the Government abroad was anxious to keep the secret patriotic organisation and network in being; indeed, the intention of sabotage passive resistance and hindrance to the Germans must have been seriously in the Czech Government's mind, should circumstances favour such activities.

The obvious first step in S.O.E. plans was to attempt proof of the Czech assertion that they had underground resources organised and in a position to act; secondly to build upon this basis if it was really found to exist. The situation and location of the Protectorate as outlined above gave communications a greater importance than almost anywhere else. This inevitably still further bound S.O.E. activities to those of "C".

At the end of January 1941, Mr F.E. Keary joined Brigadier Gubbins' staff. By this date a project had been agreed for dropping a single individual to the neighbourhood of Prague with the task of making contact with underground elements and of proving to the Czechs at home that their national interests were being watched.

In April 1941, this operation, named "Benjamin", was attempted, and the man dropped in the Protectorate. The Czechs had thus agreed to take action, with whatever reservations in their own minds. S.O.E. considered the moment had come to take an energetic line.

From May to September the R.A.F. was unable – as in subsequent years also – to undertake flights to the Protectorate. In the summer of 1941 S.O.E. pressed the Czechs to prepare action in accord with the current sabotage conceptions. That is to say: parties of 2 to 4, led by an officer or senior N.C.O., were to be dropped, accompanied by two or more 300 lb containers with a general assortment of explosives and sabotage gear and also a W/T set for communications with the United Kingdom.

This wireless traffic was throughout the War handled in the U.K. by a W/T station manned exclusively by troops under Colonel Moravec's immediate command. Until late in the War codes were purely Czech and all messages In and Out were known in the first instance only to one or two of Colonel Moravec's officers, to the Czech Minister of War and to President Beneš himself.

The 1941 period of preparation for the autumn and winter operations season was filled with a good deal of haggling about total number of Agents to be trained, nature and their intended activity – whether straight sabotage or mixed with espionage, and the possibility of pre-selecting targets.

Simultaneously the Czech Section was attempting to probe the state of Czech underground resources and disposition of worthwhile targets in and around the Protectorate. In the light of after events it appears that Colonel Moravec with his staff was reckoning up how far he must go with the appearance of undertaking sabotage in order both to look well in the eyes of the British Allies and above all to gain fresh signals facilities with the Home Country at S.O.E.'s expense.

Meetings were now frequent between Lieutenant-Colonel Wilkinson, Colonel Moravec and Major Strankmuller, Mr Keary, Lieutenant-Colonel Tichy and Major Fryc, and as occasion required between General Gubbins and General Ingr, the Minister if Defence, and indeed between General Gubbins and the more junior officers above-named.

Liaison was developed in minor matters such as exchange of information on suspected enemy agents, S.O.E. transmission of secret papers abroad for Colonel Moravec, and technical co-operation in W/T matters.

The Czechs made one exceptional contribution to S.O.E. work: in 1940 Colonel Moravec placed a Czech scientist, Dr. Malachta, at S.O.E.'s disposal. He was given a laboratory in South Kensington and aided by a gradually increasing Czech staff worked with good effect on several problems of home-made explosives, long-delay fuses, and heat chemistry.

By July 1941 the Czechs had assembled one officer and seven other ranks for the first para-military course. This began a long and happy association between Major Young at Camusdarach and a succession of Czech parties. The Czechs were found to be among the best of all S.O.E. trainees and turned out equally good parachute jumpers. Their keenness, discipline, intelligence and courage were everywhere given high praise. All this contrasted most strangely with the hanging-back, apparently wilful inefficiency, and timidity or deliberate inaction on the part of Senior Officers with whom S.O.E. dealt.

Late in the summer of 1941 the Czechs took a further decisive step by appointing Staff Captain Sustr to bear immediate responsibility for the selection, training and preparation of Czech-S.O.E. parties.

S.O.E.'s Czech office was developed into an effective and vigorous section by the addition, in September, as Operations and Training Officer, of Captain Hesketh-Pritchard, within a month or two to become Head of the Section, Mr. Keary continuing the duties of Assistant, Intelligence and Liaison Officer, and Colonel Wilkinson exercising daily guidance of Czech affairs.

By October 1941, the third Para-Military Party was in training in Scotland. Holding and accommodation for final training had become a problem. Eleven Other Ranks now underwent final operational training, largely in procedure on the ground after the parachute drop, in the use of weapons, and in preparation and laying of explosive charges. Simultaneously a house near Dorking was allotted as a Czech Operational and Holding House.

All so-called conspirative instructions and briefing for tasks on arriving Home were carried out by visiting members of Colonel Moravec's Staff. Into this instruction S.O.E. was permitted no insight. A Czech Senior Captain was posted to the Operational House. This was Captain Hrubec, who was looked on by the Czechs as O.C. Czech-S.O.E. unit. Under the vigorous impulsion of Captain Hesketh-Pritchard keen interest was developed in W/T. This led to the addition of Captain Gold as Czech Signals Officer at the school.

Chapter 3

Problems and Achievements

With the hopes of rapid dispatch to the Field, the Dorking Operational House for fifteen agents at the time appeared adequate. Headquarters Staffs for the direction of underground work were in working order on both sides in London. Equipment for agents and for sabotage purposes was rapidly being developed in great progress by S.O.E. though not yet specialised for Protectorate conditions.

The two matters which presented the greatest technical difficulties, and which were tackled by Colonel Wilkinson and Captain Hesketh-Pritchard at their appropriate levels, were air-dispatch and radio for the Field. Sustr and his junior Czech staff took an enthusiastic interest in both subjects. The flight to the Protectorate and accurate pin-pointing turned out to be amongst the most difficult task set by S.O.E. to the R.A.F. The Czech component R.A.F., at Colonel Moravec's behest, produced a complete air-crew with despatchers, which was transferred to S.O.E. flight, and there was no doubt of the success of this step.

From now on the natural S.O.E. desire to influence Czech planning for the general good, and not only to instruct but also to direct the Czech operational parties, led to a continuous struggle, largely of wits, culminating every now and again in open reproaches. Colonel Moravec carried his attitude of reserve to such lengths that at least for the first year he would not allow S.O.E.'s Czech trainees to proceed to instruction in underground and Secret Service methods nor even to advanced instruction in sabotage. This increased the difficulties of housing and occupying agents already allotted to parties, when long delays in air despatch or even the impossibility of flights became evident.

The first outstanding success was "Silver A". Although S.O.E. gained nothing tangible, the Leader, if not his No. 2, is known to have lasted from December 1941 to June or July 1942, when all signals ceased. Neither the contents of his messages nor an adequate account of his activities and fate were ever vouchsafed by Czech Headquarters.

The second effective action was the very full preparation and timely dispatch of "Anthropoid", leading to the planned execution of Heydrich on 27 May 1942 [Heydrich died of his wounds on 4 June 1942], by the two agents Kubiš and Gabčik. President Beneš is believed never to have regretted this action: there were, in any case, good grounds for the view that whilst the attack on Heydrich accelerated German action against the Czechs it did not increase the scale.

With greater deliberation, and working to Heydrich's original plan and lists, eventual German reprisals on account of prevailing dissatisfaction in the Protectorate might well have been more discriminating, and to that degree more dangerous to the patriotic cause. This is a political and general view. To S.O.E. resources in the Protectorate the result was disastrous. Almost all our S.O.E. agents despatched up till then had involved themselves in the same hide-out, the Church of St. Boromaeus in Prague, to which Kubiš and Gabčik turned for refuge, and eleven were accounted for by the Germans at one blow.

It is not known whether the loss of these valuable men through such an unpardonable error of concentration shook Colonel Moravec's faith in the effectiveness of conspirative instruction given to Agents by his own Staff Officers: at all events, by the summer of 1942 it was agreed to send Czech Trainees to our Finishing Schools.

Although the Czechs were slow to admit to S.O.E., and perhaps even to themselves, the extent of the loss suffered, Colonel Moravec and ourselves between us were now faced with the entire re-building of an underground organisation according to British ideas. Communication, that is to say, the W/T link, between the Protectorate and Britain had been totally destroyed.

Advantage was taken of the summer lull following the final April air attempts to expand and re-organise S.O.E.-Czech activities. A larger Operational House within close reach of the airfield was obtained. A sharpening of the conflict between British and Czechs for control of the School, Training and Briefing followed.

It is not necessary to emphasise the harm done to the spirit and prospects of the Agents by the circumstances of suspicion and dispute between British and Czechs which had been present from the beginning. Owing to faulty selection and composition, more than one Operational Group broke down and individual members had to be separated and allotted new tasks.

In the summer of 1942 Lieut.-Colonel Wilkinson grasped the expedient of urging Colonel Moravec to a weekly or fortnightly executive committee meeting. Full minutes were kept, and thus some check was obtained over Moravec's half-promises and the degree of their fulfilment.

To a great degree, disagreements over training and activities at the Operational House were a reflection of Colonel Moravec's dilatoriness and of the Czech Government's unsatisfactory attitude towards S.O.E.

Chapter 4

The Czech Departments

When application was made to General Ingr, in March 1942, for sabotage against the Czech railways carrying troops and material to the Russian Front, the reply was that the inevitable reprisals made such action impossible. Czech Headquarters repeated at every opportunity that the Protectorate was an unsuitable country for subversive operations, whilst claiming that their people were causing great loss to the Germans by passive resistance and undetectable sabotage.

Their objection to open activity went so far that in December 1942 Colonel Moravec said that the Czechs at home were against British aircraft even so much as flying over Protectorate territory. At the same time any information which may have been in Czech hands in London showing the state of the underground organisation or the progress of any kind of resistance to the Germans was withheld from S.O.E.

Under these circumstances of obstruction and lack of trust, preparations for operations in the season 1942/43 were set going only as the result of constant forcing from the United Kingdom.

As summer 1942 went on and the new operating season approached, matters were seen to be practically at a standstill. Parties were authorised by the Czechs one or two at a time, and always a month or more late. Apart from Moravec's political game, it was thought that full co-operation would remain exceedingly difficult as long as the sole Czech staff for S.O.E. work was a limited number of specialised intelligence officers who, moreover, had left Czechoslovakia in March 1939.

Brigadier Gubbins accordingly approached General Ingr and realised the formation of an Anglo-Czech Planning Committee which met for the first time on 23 September 1942, under Brigadier Gubbins' chairmanship. This Committee was intended by S.O.E. to control the work of Colonel Moravec's S.O.E. staff within the framework of future planning and of the project for a final national rising.

The arming and organising of underground troops in the Protectorate had gradually been thrust forward by the Czechs themselves. At all times subsequent to the turning of the tide at El Alamein and at Stalingrad, a constant influence with the Czechs was their over-optimism regarding the probable date of German submission. In this they were led by President Beneš; their talk of a national underground army and its rising as soon as Germany showed signs of weakness, began indeed, as early as 1941.

The papers laid by Czech C.H.Q. before the Anglo-Czech working committee, consisting of Lieutenant-Colonel Wilkinson and Country Section Officers, and of Colonel Moravec and his Czech S.O.E. staff, met for the first time on 5 October 1942. This Committee fulfilled its intended purpose of clearing up matters outstanding between S.O.E. and Czech H.Q. such as initiating, at least on paper, a small operational programme, agreeing on the technical preparation of one or two Parties, disposing of various difficulties at the Czech Holding House, and finally of obtaining a record of complaints which Brigadier Gubbins could lay before General Ingr.

Brigadier Gubbins' further negotiations with General Ingr in December 1942 produced the promise of a Planning Staff at Czech H.Q. This Staff had been constituted and taken over by General Miroslav by the end of January 1943.

Up till May 1943 this Staff had failed to realise the part which S.O.E. intended it to play, that is, to influence the planning and execution of Czech-S.O.E. operations in accordance with long-term requirements and not merely as decided by Colonel Moravec. It had at most become a potential source of air and tactical and other relevant intelligence.

On the other hand, Moravec's hand was forced by the whole proceeding. An officer of field rank took over Czech-S.O.E. affairs at Moravec's Headquarters, and by 12 February 1943, S.O.E. had received the first Czech proposal for the provisional employment of all the men at the Operational and Holding House some of whom had been on S.O.E. books for 9-15 months.

S.O.E. financial relations with the Czech Government coincided with the precedent set by "C", and the Lease-Lend Agreement of 21 February 1943, between British and Czech Government did not alter the previous arrangements, by which Czech H.Q. paid only for foreign currency, for special transport facilities such as air passage, for civilian clothing bought in an emergency for operational or other purposes, and a monthly subvention to the S. Kensington Laboratory.

Chapter 5

Activities in the Field

After Heydrich's execution on 27 May 1942, we did not hear of any positive S.O.E. contribution to the war effort in Czechoslovakia.

"Silver A" kept signals going until mid-June 1942. The village of Lezaky was destroyed by the Germans following "Silver A" Leader's stay there, and his escape from a German raiding party under cover of resistance by the inhabitants.

In May 1943, the surviving member of "Antimony", landed on 14 October 1942, was still in possession of his W/T transmitter, with which he was signalling for one hour on each of two days in the week. Czech H.Q. asserted that he was in contact with an organisation in N. Bohemia, and that he was signalling back safe addresses. "Antimony" appears to have carried a compromising and somewhat anti-Allied letter from Dr. Beneš, and to have allowed it to fall into German hands.

There can be no doubt that security measures against parachutists and against subversive stirrings which might follow their arrival caused the Germans to employ considerable personnel and organisation.

Chapter 6

The 1942–1943 Season

With the developments outlined previously, S.O.E. was already in a better position to follow the new C.O.S. Directive of 20 March 1943. This stated the following

Poland and Czechoslovakia
The sabotage of German communications to the Russian front in these areas is of primary importance. The preparation of forces to take organised military action when the German hold is weakened has great political importance in these countries. Such forces will undoubtedly yield valuable results when the time comes, but the supply of equipment for them should not be allowed to interfere to too great extent with the provision of material for sabotage which can be carried out now.

Early in 1943 there was a re-organisation within the direction of S.O.E. which brought Poland, Czechoslovakia and Hungary into one Region under Lt-Colonel H.B. Perkins. He had never given up hope that something could be done in Czechoslovakia, despite the disappointing record and the many altercations which had taken place between the two H.Q.s, and in spite of opposition, which mooted the closing down of the Czech Section managed to carry his point, and succeeded in obtaining a reprieve for long enough to have another try to get agents infiltrated and communications restored.

Accordingly, one party of four was selected from the thirty-odd students whom we then had at our disposal, and they were sent down to the Despatch School at Station 19 with a view to dropping them near Pilsen; the intention was to drop them as a sort of "test case" in order to find out if it were possible to exist in Czechoslovakia and maintain satisfactory communications. At the same time the remaining students were divided up into parties and were given further training at S.T.S. 46.

It must be remembered that at the same time "C" were undergoing the same trouble which we were experiencing, and also were having no success, so they were just as much interested in the result of our operation as we were.

This party, whose code name was "Sulphur" (Mercury) underwent three months of the most trying conditions, and although suitable high priority had been obtained for them with the R.A.F., everything appeared to be against them. There were only two days in each month when it was possible to attempt the long journey to Czechoslovakia and back, and on each occasion something cropped up to make the sortie unsuccessful. In all they made seven attempts, the aircraft reaching the dropping area on four occasions, but weather, flak and lack of knowledge of the target (it must be remembered that this was a "blind drop") always prevented the operation being carried out. The lack of success of this operation was a great strain on the morale of the party, and eventually the leader and second in command quarrelled, and the party was reduced to three. Attempts were made until the end of March, by which time the season was ended until the following autumn.

Occupational Scheme

To tide over the summer non-operational period, occupation was found for our operators by giving them technical courses in Government Training Centres. Clandestine living conditions, underground activities and concealed W/T operation were all practiced throughout this four months' training period. Concurrently with this training scheme, preparations were being made at S.O.E. and Czech H.Q. for all future flights to Poland and Czechoslovakia to be carried out from a forward base in Italy, and with this end in view all parties were appropriately trained and equipped. About this time also our relations with "C" began to improve; it was realised that as the few students available were obviously to be divided between ourselves and "C", and intended to exchange the personnel of the parties just as he liked, better relations with "C" would have to be effected if any tangible and concrete results were to be achieved.

There was also the question of W/T communications; apart from the fact that it was intended that the parties in the Field should communicate with the U.K. to the "C" W/T station at Hockliffe, they were also being equipped with roughly 50% S.I.S. equipment and 50% S.O.E. Moreover, both S.O.E. and S.I.S. parties were being trained in W/T procedure by "C", using their own equipment, so close and amicable liaison was absolutely essential.

Thus, it came about that a member of an S.O.E. party might find himself in an S.O.E. mission one week and being transferred to S.I.S. the next. In addition to this, of course, briefing was done solely by Czechoslovak H.Q., who were advised by us and pleased themselves whether they acted upon our advice or not.

This system, however, suited our particular ends fairly well, as before any S.O.E. task could possibly be given or carried out it was vitally essential that good and accurate intelligence should be received first. Furthermore, as most of the students had already been trained in S.O.E. work prior to their posting to S.I.S., we had every hope that the more active work in which we specialised would take precedence when they actually arrived in the Field. This, in fact, turned out to be the case when the parties finally were delivered to the Field, as most of the intelligence parties spent a great deal of their time organising Reception Committees and receiving stores when, in fact, their tasks were purely intelligence.

The Operational Season 1943-1944
By the end of the summer 1943, all preparations had been made for future operations to be carried out from our Italian base, although the equipping and briefing of all parties were to be done in London.

This system worked extremely well, in spite of the great distance between the U.K. and Italy, the communications were excellent, and after the disappointing season which we had experienced in 1942/43, both Czechoslovak H.Q. and ourselves looked forward much more optimistically to the coming season.

Chapter 7

Operations from the Mediterranean Theatre

September 1943 to April 1945

The situation in Czechoslovakia prior to the commencement of operations from Mediterranean Theatre was as follows:

1. From 1941 onwards a few Czech parties had been infiltrated from the U.K. and had established communication with the resistance movement in Czechoslovakia which was then being formed. Their tasks were to help in co-ordinating this movement, to assist in building up the underground organisation, and to establish communications with the Czech authorities in England.

    In the Spring of 1942, Heydrich, the "Protector" of Bohemia and Moravia, was murdered. Heydrich had been responsible for the atrocities which had been perpetrated in the country and was the Gestapo officer second in command to Himmler. A large-scale drive was then instituted by the Germans in the Protectorate with the object of crushing any potential resistance movement. In the course of this drive, they were successful in disrupting entirely our organisation and communications. One of the well known examples of this drive was "Lidice" for having sheltered "Silver A" with his W/T set.

2. Between this time and the start of our operations from the Mediterranean the resistance movement was re-organising slowly in the field but was out of touch with the Czech authorities in London and it lacked direction. Our main objective therefore was

to send in parties to Czechoslovakia to help in the re-organisation of the resistance movement under the control of the Czech Government to reopen communications and to establish a network of reception committees for future work. These parties were also to provide as much intelligence as possible on the state of resistance inside the country.

Under these circumstances it was imperative for us to infiltrate our trained parties as quickly as possible, and each party was allotted a particular area of the country in which it was to work. This plan was finally carried out and the organisation of reception committees by areas was arranged. The stores operations which were finally sent to these areas went under the code name of "Ely". The parties whom we sent in carried out their work admirably and in the East the plan worked well, but in other parts of the country events moved too rapidly for us to put into effect the entire plan as it was originally conceived.

Transfer of Operations from U.K. to the Mediterranean
3. In the winter of 1943 the hazards of flying to Czechoslovakia from the U.K. became too great owing to German night fighter opposition and flak and it was decided that special operations to that country should be carried out from the Mediterranean. The previous route used from England was the Southern one and the aircraft used to pinpoint on Lake Constance and then go on to Czechoslovakia.

From Lake Constance onwards there were no good pinpoints and the weather had to be extremely good in order to give the slightest chance of success. This entailed making flights only during the full moon period when the danger from fighter aircraft was at its highest. The result of these difficult flying conditions was that very few parties had been infiltrated to Czechoslovakia and that communications with that country were in a fairly poor state. It was decided by the Air Ministry that a squadron of eighteen four-engined aircraft be allotted in the Mediterranean Theatre for the conduct of special operations to Czechoslovakia and Poland. Twelve of the aircraft were to be manned by Polish crews who would fly from England to the Mediterranean Base and the ground staff for these was to be Polish. The remaining six aircraft were to be provided out of local resources.

At that time there were three Polish manned Liberator aircraft in 138 Squadron in the U.K. and the Poles were pressing for the Mediterranean Squadron to be composed of Liberators instead of Halifaxes which were normally used.

Sorties from North Africa

4. The possibility of flying form the Mediterranean had been first considered in September 1943. During that month four Czech parties, namely "Sulphur", "Chalk", "Carbon" and "Clay" were taken to Massingham with a view to flying them to Czechoslovakia by staging at Sidi Amor or Malta.

   Two attempts were in fact made unsuccessfully from Malta and the parties returned to Massingham where they remained in charge of the Czech Conducting Officer, Captain Hajny (Hrubec). No further operations to Czechoslovakia were attempted from North Africa and in December an operational base was established in Italy.

Provision of Airlift, Italy

5. The Air Ministry's direction for the provision of 18 aircraft was at this time not fulfilled and the promised Squadron consisting of 18 aircraft was in fact only one Flight whose number was 1586. This Flight, together with 148 Squadron made up the heavy bomber complement of 334 Wing which from December 1943 onwards was based on Brindisi.

   Although the task of 1586 Flight was to carry out operations to Poland and Czechoslovakia, whereas 148 Squadron's task was to carry out operations to the remainder of the countries served by S.O.M., it was decided to make a local agreement that 1586 Flight should fly to Northern Italy, Yugoslavia, Greece, etc., when weather conditions were not possible for flying to Czechoslovakia and Poland and in exchange when weather was favourable 148 Squadron should send aircraft to these two countries.

The hoped-for Liberators did not materialise except for the three which flew out from the U.K. and the remainder of the aircraft were Halifaxes. At the end of December two of the Liberators crashed and were destroyed making the aircraft position particularly bad. It had been hoped that the weather in Southern Italy would be favourable but this was not the case and it was not until April 8th that we were able to carry out a Czech operation.

Operations 1944

6. Our first operation from Italy was carried out on 8 April 1944. On that date "Sulphur" and "Chalk" parties consisting of two and four men respectively were dropped successfully into Czechoslovakia, the "Chalk" party flashing their safe arrival from the ground.

The following day, i.e. 9 April, parties "Carbon" and "Clay" consisting respectively of four and three men made an abortive sortie and returned unsuccessfully owing to bad weather. They tried again on the 12th, however, and landed successfully, "Carbon" flashing its safe arrival from the ground. No more operations were carried out until 9 June when "Manganese", consisting of three nationals dropped successfully to Slovakia but unfortunately lost part of their W/T equipment.

Another gap in our operations occurred until July 3rd when "Glucinium", a party consisting of four Czechs, was dropped. They fell partly in a wood; all their material was destroyed and the party captured with the exception of its leader who managed to get away. Except for an unsuccessful supply operation to "Chalk" on 18 July no further operations were attempted until 13 September when "Wolfram", a party of six nationals with legbags, were dropped successfully but their W/T operator unfortunately later fell into German hands.

The main reason for this gap in Czech operations was that the rising in Warsaw was at that time taking place and an overriding priority had been given by London that when conditions were suitable a maximum effort should be made to Poland. As weather conditions in the two countries coincided the result was that despite occasional good weather no operations at all were attempted to Czechoslovakia for a period of nearly two months.

Slovak Rising

7. On 4 July 1944, London warned us by telegram that preparations were being made for a rising in Slovakia to be concentrated in the Banska Bystrica area. They had received a rough estimate from the field of stores which would be required and we were asked to make the necessary provision. The plan for this rising was that two Czech Divisions then located at Prešov and Vihorlat were to march towards Banska Bystrica whilst reserve troops in this area were to support the revolting divisions.

We were asked to be prepared to supply the reserve troops but were informed that the regular forces would be in possession of sufficient arms and material. An officer had already been appointed by London to take charge of the rising.

On 31 August we were informed that this rising had taken place. It had been precipitated by the decision of the Germans to occupy the whole of Slovakia as a defence measure against the Russians.

8. The two divisions of the Slovak Army mentioned above started to fight their way through the Carpathians towards the Russians and also towards Banska Bystrica. At the same time the Germans advanced in force and were eventually successful in preventing the main forces of the regular Slovak Divisions from joining the troops fighting in the neighbourhood of Banska Bystrica. Our party "Manganese" was reporting on the situation from the Headquarters of the Commander of the rising, General Golian. Negotiations were still in progress in London for permission for us to send supplies.

These negotiations in the end proved fruitless as it was decided that the Russians should give all the necessary support with the exception of certain medical supplies which we were asked to send. The partisans and a few regular troops at that time under the control of General Golian were then in possession of airfields at Tri Duby and Mokrad in the area of Ružomberok and fighting had become general in Western and Central Slovakia. The Slovaks were carrying out sabotage of German transport and communications. The transmitting station at Banska Bystrica was in Slovak hands and broadcast regularly until destroyed by German aerial attack about 5 September.

9. On 6 September the Russians delivered equipment by landing 30 transport planes and also sent a contingent of the Czech Parachute Brigade numbering some 700 officers and men. They also landed 24 fighters manned by Czechs which were left at Tri Duby to assist in the fighting. At this time the Slovaks controlled an area in Central Slovakia within a radius of 40 or 50 miles of Banska Bystrica which was the main centre of the revolt and the Headquarters of General Golian.

The Germans had marshalled 4 Divisions against the Slovaks. On 17 September, the 15th U.S.A.A.F. landed two Fortresses at Tri Duby airfield under the escort of 41 fighters. This they did in order to pick up some stranded U.S. airmen but at the same time they took in material to support the rising.

The 15th U.S.A.A.F. intended to make another sortie later on to take in more stores and some personnel and to exfiltrate the remainder of the stranded U.S. airmen. We asked permission for the "Windproof" party to be taken in on this sortie if they had not been infiltrated before it took place. "Windproof" did in fact drop to Slovakia before this second American sortie. See report on "Windproof".

10. When we heard that this second American sortie might take place Lieutenant-Colonel Threlfall asked permission from London to be allowed to go in and find out the situation from General Golian and come out again on the same sortie. Permission was granted and London telegraphed that they would like to send Lieutenant-Colonel Souhrada to accompany him but to remain with General Golian.

They also said that they would like some Slovak personnel to be exfiltrated. This was arranged and on 7 October operation "Quartz" was successfully attempted.

11. On the night of 5 October a Czech General named Viest was sent in from Russia to take over the command of the rising which was by then not going to well as the Germans were closing in on the Slovak held area. Our London Headquarters had sent us two officers Majors Greenlees and Raw with their W/T operators for infiltration to General Golian but owing to the deteriorating situation their operation did not take place.

On 25 October we had a report from the field that Brezno and Zvollen had fallen and that the capture of Tri Duby airfield was imminent. After that contact with the field was broken.

The German controlled Bratislava radio announced the capture of Generals Viest and Golian on 4 November. We were later informed by "Windproof" that General Golian had given orders for the Slovak soldiers to return to their homes and that the remnants of the Czech Brigade and those Slovaks who were compromised took to the forest in bands. The American and British parties also dispersed. Any further news we have of them is contained in the report on "Windproof".

"Windproof"

12. During the whole of the Slovak rising our party "Manganese" had been used for maintaining contact with General Golian. They were in need of extra W/T supplies and these were sent them with a British party called "Windproof" consisting of four members headed by Major Sehmer.

"Windproof" was sent to Slovakia by the Hungarian Section, with full agreement of the Slovaks, for infiltration overland into Hungary. They had been waiting either for one of the American landing sorties to take them to Tri Duby, or if a fine night occurred sooner to drop to Tri Duby airfield. They finally dropped with "Manganese" supplies on September 18th and the pilot reported the success of the operation. We did not hear anything from them for some days but when they did come on the air, they informed us that they had been dropped 30 miles away from their pinpoint and within a very short distance of the German lines but had managed to walk to Banska Bystrica.

On arrival there Major Sehmer discussed his position with General Golian who informed that it would be difficult to proceed immediately to Hungary owing to the confused situation and German activity at the moment. "Windproof" therefore stayed at General Golian's Headquarters and became extremely useful as an extra W/T link.

It had previously been expressly explained to Sehmer that he had no official function in Czechoslovakia and that he had gone there solely as a jumping off point for this mission to Hungary. Sehmer made this clear to General Golian but nevertheless the Slovaks felt that they wanted some British representation in order to stress the Allied backing that they were enjoying, and so published in their local newspapers that Major Sehmer had been sent as head of a British mission to them. His position was extremely difficult, and London pressed him to continue his journey to Hungary immediately if possible. This he could not do for the time being, but sent a Hungarian speaking member of his party, namely Daniels, into Hungary to make a reconnaissance and obtain papers and safe addresses to which the whole "Windproof" party could go.

Later on Sehmer and the other two members of his party, Willis and Zenopian, set off for the Hungarian border. This journey coincided with a German drive and they were cut off. They tried to return to Banska Bystrica but found this impossible so took to the hills where they came across a small partisan unit whom they joined. They lived for some time with this unit and then transferred to a slightly larger one. They later came across an American O.S.S. group headed by Captain Green who had got away from Banska Bystrica after the collapse of the Slovak rising and were in hiding near the village of Polomka.

As well as the members of the O.S.S. mission, Captain Green had with him a number of baled out American airmen. Major

Sehmer and Captain Green joined forces although not living in the same house.

The "Windproof" house was on a hillside, Captain Green's being considerably lower down. Although "Windproof" was in touch with us by W/T his batteries had failed through lack of generating power and he and his operator were forced to go down to the village of Polomka when they wished to transmit. This village was full of German soldiers and therefore transmission was an extremely risky business. They were also suffering from lack of food and clothing and we had prepared a relief sortie for them.

The weather was bad but on 21 October we made our first attempt to supply them but the aircraft run into a storm and had to jettison its load. "Windproof" said that they were only waiting near Polomka to receive our sortie and wanted to join a large group of partisans under the command of Colonel Prykril some distance away immediately the operation was successful.

Unfortunately, it was not until 21 December that we were able to make another attempt which was also unsuccessful due to the aircraft icing up. Another attempt was made on 27 December which was thought to be successful but it subsequently turned out that the load had been dropped to a Russian reception committee in the district. At this time, we were quite out of touch with "Windproof", their last message to us being transmitted on 16 December.

It was imperative that we should take drastic measures to get in touch with them again without having to wait for one of the extremely rare fine nights, so we investigated the possibility of putting hand and pedal generators into the jettison tanks of a fighter aircraft and making a daylight sortie. One such sortie was carried out by two fighters on 21 January and they reported that they had dropped their jettison tanks just by the house at which the Americans re said to be living.

We heard no news from the field and were extremely worried. On 24 January 1945, the German controlled Bratislava radio made an announcement as follows:

18 members of a group of Anglo-U.S. agents led by an American named Green and an Englishman called Sehmer, who pretended to be a Major, were captured by a Hungarian party in the rear of the German sector, so competent German quarters announce. The interrogation revealed that it was their task to carry out economic and political espionage for the Anglo-Americans and commit acts of sabotage in Slovakia. These agents, who were wearing civilian clothes when seized, were sentenced to death by Court Martial and were shot.

13. London informed us that they had heard this announcement but could not check its veracity and were not sure whether or not it was a blind.

    One of the "Windproof" party, namely Zenopian, has since come to Italy and told us the story of what happened on 26 December. He says that Sehmer and Willis, both in uniform were visiting Captain Green at his house lower down the mountainside, when the Germans appeared and arrested them and took the whole party away. He says that some of the Americans were visiting the "Windproof" house and that he and they got wind of the approach of the Germans and managed to escape before their arrival. The Russians have recently informed London that they have definite proof that Sehmer and the others were definitely shot by the Germans.

"Mica"

14. In October London sent us a party called "Mica" consisting of Majors Greenlees and Raw and a Czech officer Major Schweitzer together with their W/T operators. They were to be infiltrated to General Golian as an official British mission to supersede "Windproof".

    The rising collapsed before this was possible. London then informed us that "Mica" should wait in Italy to be infiltrated to Czechoslovakia later with a fresh task. This however never materialised and they went back to the U.K. in January, when their places were filled by Majors Forster and Seymour who arrived from the U.K.

"Silica" – Czech Troops in Northern Italy

15. In August 1944 our Headquarters in London were interesting themselves in the Czechoslovak troops under German control who were then stationed in Northern Italy. These troops were deserting in some numbers and were said to be fairly well organised and willing to come over to the Allies if given the opportunity.

We informed London that any action connected with these troops must be effected through the medium of the Italian section as they were the co-ordinating body under the direction of A.F.H.Q. for any project put forward in connection with Northern Italy. Mr Keary was sent out by London Headquarters to co-ordinate the projects they had conceived for subverting the Czech troops.

Two parties were prepared, "Silica" South whose members were Lieutenant-Colonel Cope, Captain Havel (a Czech officer) and their W/T operator Corporal Williamson, and "Silica" North composed of Major Whitaker, Captain Hajny (a Czech officer) and a Czech W/T operator named Nocar. "Silica" North was attempted unsuccessfully on the 8 October and "Silica" South was dropped successfully to the Turin area on 9 September.

"Silica" North was again attempted on 11 October, but the aircraft did not return. Subsequent reports from the field caused us to assume that the aircraft crashed into a mountain near the dropping area and that all the occupants were killed.

16. All information previously obtained had led us to believe that there was a great number of Czechoslovaks in the Turin area. After we had dropped "Silica" South and they had made their initial reconnaissance it was found that the Czechs had moved out of the area a short time previously and had gone to the Milan area.

It became impossible for "Silica" to move to the Milan area as the Czech units were situated in the plains which were closely controlled by the Germans. Several plans were made for getting in touch with the Czechs at their new location but in the end these all came to nothing and the only solution was to withdraw the party. Cope and Havel were picked up by Lysander from an Italian Section landing ground on 18 November, at the request of the Italian Section their operator, Corporal Williamson, was transferred to their section and left to continue his work in the field.

17. After the disaster to "Silica" North and the revelations that there were no Czech troops in the "Silica" South area, London proposed to send further personnel with a view to contacting Czech units in other parts of Northern Italy.

Every effort was made to try and organise further operations but A.A.I. who allotted all air priorities for Northern Italy were not prepared to consider allowing us further sorties for the purpose of Czech subversion and the plan had to be dropped.

Summary of Operations in 1944

18. By the end of 1944 we had carried out from Italy a total of 22 sorties to Czechoslovakia of which 10 were successful. We had dropped 30 men and 9000 lbs of stores. 15 of the sorties had been carried out by 148 Squadron and the remaining 7 by 1586 Flight, which later became 301 Squadron.

The situation of our parties in the field at the end of 1944 together with their names and the areas in which they were working is given in Appendix A.

Operations in 1945

19. Since May 1944 we had been holding a party of four Czechs whose code name was "Platinum". Czech Headquarters were most anxious that they should go to the Protectorate and various attempts were made to infiltrate them, on 4 October, 21 December and finally on 16 February 1945, when their operation was successful.

Unfortunately, they damaged the W/T material which they took in their leg bags However one set still worked and they could communicate with London with the crystals that remained intact. This party worked extremely well, and we later sent them further crystals and W/T material but satisfactory contact was never established with Italy although their communications with London worked well. Subsequently this party split into two, one group remaining in E. Bohemia and the other group of two going to Prague.

Together with "Tungsten", an S.I.S. party, they organised many reception committees and helped to give Czech Headquarters and our Headquarters in London a clearer picture of what was going on and were also able to receive instructions from them. They were in constant touch with the U.K. throughout the Protectorate Rising which is described later in this report.

20. In 1945 only one more man was infiltrated his operation being named "Bauxite". After three unsuccessful attempts this Czech agent dropped to the "Tungsten" reception committee on the Bohemian Moravian border and established good contact with us almost immediately afterwards but was unable to achieve satisfactory W/T communication with London. He did exceptionally good work in attempting to improve the organisation of the reception committees in his area, and was later the channel through which messages from the Czech National Council in Moravia were passed to us. These messages are referred to late in this report.

21. One more Czech party called "Foursquare", consisting of four Czechs was sent to Italy by London but we were never able to infiltrate them from here. Finally, they were flown to Dijon in an operational aircraft which was going to continue its journey to Czechoslovakia from there in the hope that weather conditions would be more favourable. This party made one unsuccessful sortie over the target during which firing was seen on the ground but no reception committee. They were later taken back to the U.K. by their accompanying officer Captain Panter.

22. Major Forster and Seymour and their W/T operators Sergeant Edwards and Sergeant Roberts had been waiting to go to Czechoslovakia since they took over from "Mica" in January 1945. They planned to drop to "Platinum" or "Bauxite" on reception of

news from either party that conditions were suitable for British officers to operate.

In April "Bauxite" signalled that he was prepared to receive them. A spell of bad weather followed, and events were moving fast. As in the case of "Foursquare", London now decided that "Pigotite", as their mission was then called, should go nearer the approach of the American armies and should drop in Western Bohemia. They made one unsuccessful sortie and then the weather prevented any further attempts until hostilities ceased.

23. As previously mentioned, the general plan governing operations to Czechoslovakia was firstly to drop organising parties to specific areas and then to send supplies to the receptions they set up. The code name "Ely" was allotted to these supply drops as a whole. In February 1945 we carried out the first of these stores drops with standard supplies of arms, ammunition and explosives and continued them until operations ceased.

Protectorate Rising

24. In September 1944 we were informed by London that they were approaching the Chiefs of Staff with a view to considering the question of the promotion of an armed uprising in the Protectorate of Czechoslovakia. We were to investigate the possibility of arming 10,500 men in the nearest future and the possibility of arming 50,000 men at a later date and maintaining them after the outbreak of the rising.

We informed London that supplying 10,500 men would be possible but that supplies were not adequate for arming and maintaining the further 50,000 unless definite instructions were received from the Chiefs of Staff making the necessary airlift and equipment available. In October our London H.Q. informed us that the Czechs had approached the Chiefs of Staff putting forward the plan mentioned above.

After consultation with the Foreign Office and S.O.E. the Chiefs of Staff informed the Czechoslovak Government that the project was not feasible and gave as reasons for their adverse decision:

(a) that Czechoslovakia was not included in the Anglo-American theatre of operations.
(b) that from past experience, both British and German, i.e. Stalingrad, Tunis, Arnhem, and Warsaw, it was shown that support by air of isolated land forces proved impossible.
(c) the adverse weather conditions for flying to Czechoslovakia which would prevail during the period when help would be most required.

25. S.O.E. and the Foreign Office indicated to the Chiefs of Staff their moral responsibility for giving assistance to resistance movements in Bohemia and Moravia which had been formed at our instigation. The Chiefs of Staff agreed to grant support of sabotage and guerilla activities on a small scale on a definite understanding with the Czechs that a large-scale rising could in no way be equipped or maintained.

We were instructed to earmark equipment for 10,500 men, provision arrangements for which had already been made for the support of these activities. After the Russian winter offensive at the beginning of 1945 their front line was fairly static near the borders of the Protectorate. We were therefore given pinpoints in Moravia, to which supplies were to be sent as it was the intention to build up the resistance movement there in order to sabotage German communications.

Owing to weather conditions we were not able to carry out very many operations during the winter but when the weather improved a number of sorties were made to these pinpoints. The semi-trained reception committees were in some cases not sufficiently experienced, and a considerable number of ineffective sorties were made. The field was meanwhile pressed to improve its reception arrangements.

26. Later on the Russians began to advance and we were instructed to step up our activity. The question then arose of the proximity of the Russian line to certain reception committees. We were continually

asked by 15 Army Group, who controlled all sorties made by the Squadrons working for us, to give them up to date information:

(a) of the Russian line
(b) of the situation in the field.

27. We asked London for guidance but they seemed to be nearly as much in the dark as we ourselves regarding the actual position of the Russians and their information when it reached us was often a little out of date. As neither they nor we were in touch with all individual reception committees and movement in the field was restricted, our information as to the non-receptions and information regarding what we thought to be successful sorties was considerably delayed.

Despite the lack of information, we were able to give to 15 Army Group and the Squadrons concerned, they were still prepared to fly to reception points where no lights had been seen. A little later however their attitude stiffened slightly, and they were no longer prepared to fly twice to a point at which there had been no reception unless we had definite news from the field that the reception committee was in fact standing by.

A number of reception points in Moravia became to near to the front line and we were informed that we would have to choose points further West. This we did and when the American 3rd Army made its spectacular advance to the borders of Bohemia, we prepared to supply receptions in the Prague-Pilsen area in addition to those in Eastern Bohemia and Moravia.

At this juncture it had been the intention to send Majors Forster and Seymour and their W/T operators, under the code name "Pigotite", to join "Bauxite" in Eastern Bohemia. "Foursquare", a party of four Czechs was also going to this area. However, owing to the rapid advance of General Patton's forces London instructed us to send these parties further West and "Pigotite" did make one sortie to Western Bohemia but instead of a reception committee, firing on the ground was observed.

Weather conditions then held up operations for some days and whilst a new pinpoint was being sought for "Pigotite", "Foursquare" went in their operational aircraft to Dijon accompanied by Captain Panter, as the met. forecast showed that there would be a better possibility of flying from Dijon during the next few days than there would be from Rosignano. "Foursquare" made one unsuccessful attempt from Dijon but "Pigotite" was not able to try again before hostilities ceased and we were instructed to stop further flights.

28. During the critical period when both the Russian and American Armies were advancing, communications with Moravia and Eastern Bohemia were disrupted owing to the stoppage of the electrical supply in that area for the ten days ending 29 April.

This considerably interrupted our work. From then on, many messages came in from "Bauxite" who was in control of a number of reception points in the area stressing their dire need, and the urgency of supplying them immediately. The Germans were instituting drives and attacking them but they had insufficient arms to put up effective opposition. Our last successful sortie was on 25 April and from that date until 9 May, when we were told to cease all operations, we had not been able to carry out any operations from Italy owing to an extraordinary stretch of bad weather.

29. During this time "Bauxite" was stationed with the Military Representative of the Czech National Council in Moravia. His messages grew more and more insistent, and the situation became extremely strained as he and the people with whom he was stationed were unable to understand our inability to supply them when their need was too patently obvious.

In one of his telegrams "Bauxite" said that the people with whom he was were sure, "That former unfortunate Munich repeat Munich is repeated from the West."

His penultimate message transmitted at 12.59 hours GMT on 8 May finished by saying:

We are hearing from you only excuses as weather or front line. This is our last desperate try. If not successful will be forced to finish with you. Please inform London. Expecting reply at 16, 17, 18, 19 hrs skeds today. Signed Military Representative of Czech National Council in Moravia. Josepp.

30. At 1745 hours on the same day he sent his last message saying:

> Please for God's sake do your best tonight, and tomorrow night. Its worse than hell here. Great required operation on Ambrolny rpt Ambrolny expecting tomorrow night. Reply urgently in sked Josefs.

Since that message we have not heard from "Bauxite". The unfortunate turn in the weather when we were not able to conduct a single flight between 25 April and 9 May may have left a false impression with the patriots of Moravia and Bohemia which it will take much to dispel.

Summary of Operations in 1945
31. From January 1945 until the cessation of hostilities in May we carried out 101 sorties of which only 23 were successful. Five men and 83,121 lbs of stores were dropped during this period.

Summary of Czech Operations From Italy
32. During the period in which operations to Czechoslovakia were conducted from Italy, i.e., from December 1943 until May 1945, the following results were achieved:

Total number of sorties:	123
Successful:	33
Unsuccessful:	90
Bodies dropped:	35
Missions infiltrated:	10
Total weight of stores in tons	41

Sorties flown by British crews:
Successful: 14
Unsuccessful: 18

Sorties flown by Polish crews:
Successful: 6
Unsuccessful: 18

Sorties flown by American crews:
Successful: 13
Unsuccessful: 54

Structure of the Czech Section

33. The Czech Section in Italy began in December 1944 as a part of "Torment", an organisation set up to conduct operations chiefly to Poland but also to Czechoslovakia.

Lieutenant-Colonel Roper-Caldbeck was the officer in charge of "Torment" with Major A.M. Morgan as his chief operations officer. Two holding houses at Laureto were set aside for Czech personnel who were under the care of their Czech conducting officer Captain Hajny. F.A.N.Y personnel did the administration and catering. Soon after Lieutenant M.F. Drake, a Czech speaking British officer, was taken on to assist in the running of the Section.

34. In April 1944, Lieutenant-Colonel H.M. Threlfall and Major G.I. Klauber were sent out by London, and Force 139 was established with Lieutenant-Colonel Threlfall as its Commander, to interpret London's policy for the conduct of operations to Poland, Czechoslovakia and Hungary.

The Headquarters of Force 139 was established at Monopoli and Lieutenant Drake was shortly replaced by Lieutenant D.F. Thomas. In September, Lieutenant Thomas returned to London and was replaced by Captain P.H.J. Panter who was sent out by our Headquarters.

35. At all times, London controlled the policy to be adopted for operations to Czechoslovakia, but Force 139 were responsible,

under their direction, for forward planning for provision of airlift, stores, signals material and communications through the medium of S.O.M.

Move of H.Q. S.O.M. to Siena
36. In March 1945, H.Q. S.O.M. moved from Southern Italy to Siena. S.O.M. units in the South had stretched over the countryside from Bari to Brindisi and it was decided to concentrate the whole Headquarters staff as well as the country sections staff under one roof. This entailed a certain amount of streamlining and Force 139 amongst other units was disbanded, the Czech Section being incorporated in H.Q. S.O.M. under the title of M.3. Section with Major Klauber in charge.

Effect of Move to Siena on Czech Operations
37. Until the end of March, Czech operations had been carried out by the British and Polish Heavy Bomber Squadrons of 334 Wing stationed at Brindisi. When S.O.M. moved, it had been found necessary to choose an airfield in the Siena area and Rosignano was the one decided upon.

Accordingly, a Czech holding and despatch house in the neighbourhood of Rosignano was chosen to accommodate the Czech and British parties then in Italy, and the further Czech parties expected from the U.K. The airfield and holding house were some two to two and a half hours drive from Siena and telephone and D.R. communication were at first bad. S.O.M. had no Packing Station on the lines of M.E. 54 in the Rosignano area, but instead they established a dump of packed containers nearby at Cecina.

These containers were packed at M.E.54 and sent to Cecina ready for air transport. O.S.S. had a packing station nearby which was ready to assist in packing any special loads. Also, a small detachment was sent from M.E.54 to assist in this work.

It is noteworthy to mention here that both M.E.54 and the S.O.M. Q Ops Unit at Cecina were at all times most helpful in packing special loads for the Czech Section in the shortest possible time, and so facilitated our work in laying on any non-standard operations called for by the Field.

Changeover to American Airforce

38. The most noticeable effect in our change of location was that operations to Czechoslovakia were henceforth undertaken by American instead of British and Polish aircrews.

Day to day priorities down South had been allotted by B.A.F. in consultation with 334 Wing who controlled 148 and 301, the Squadrons concerned. The R.A.F. and Polish Airforce personnel were all well acquainted with our problems and understood the task we had to perform. From Siena priorities were controlled by 15 Army Group in conjunction with 2641 Bomb Group (Prov.) who controlled 885 and 859, the squadrons working for us.

Although all concerned were keen and anxious to do their best for us, they naturally wanted to be fully informed and to be given as complete a picture as possible of the constantly changing situation in the Field. We did our best to pass on all relevant information, but we ourselves lacked detailed news from time to time. Nevertheless, the Americans gave us their fullest support and, as results show, succeeded in substantially increasing the average number of sorties flown.

Liaison with O.S.S

39. In London our Czech Section was more or less integrated with that of O.S.S. In Italy, whilst operations were conducted from Brindisi, the O.S.S. Czech Section was situated in Bari while S.O.E.'s Czech Section was in Monopoli.

At first liaison was established on a high level but later on liaison was good throughout both departments and resulted in our keeping O.S.S. fully informed of all activities in the Field, whilst they reciprocated. O.S.S. were not very interested on the S.O. angle of work into Czechoslovakia but concentrated more on the S.I. side.

Our relations were so good towards the end of our stay in Monopoli that they asked us to arrange with the Field Receptions for their parties and allowed themselves to be largely dependent on us for the organisation of their sorties. When our section moved to Siena, the O.S. Czech Section synchronised their move to the Rosignano area and our collaboration continued as before until such time as their Czech Section was moved from the Mediterranean Theatre of Operations and put under ETOUSA.

Liaison with I.S.L.D.
40. Liaison was established early with I.S.L.D. who had no real Czech Section in Italy. They acted purely as a holding and despatch establishment for their London Headquarters. London sent them agents, usually with an accompanying officer, and this accompanying officer was in charge of the operation until it was completed when he would return to the U.K. I.S.L.D. out here were not fully informed of events in Czechoslovakia. In certain instances, we were charged with the re-supply of their parties in the Field.

Liaison with P.W.B.
41. We were in touch with P.W.B. who established an office in Bari dealing with Czech matters, after they had consulted our London H.Q and our Czech Section here. We lent them an officer to assist in monitoring broadcasts from Czechoslovakia.

Liaison with "A" Force (I.S.9)
42. Liaison was established early with A Force and one of their agents, namely Willis, went to Slovakia with the "Windproof" party. They gave us all the news they had of the situation in Slovakia and we also kept them fully informed. We had periodical exchanges of information and helped one another from time to time by way of special stores.

Liaison with Air Forces

43. Our liaison with B.A.F who were in control of the aircraft flying from Brindisi was close and friendly in fact liaison with the Air Force right the way through was most cordial. They made our work much easier and gave us the utmost possible help, even in so far as to allow our Czech Liaison Officer to be present at the interrogation of the crews when they returned from flights to Czechoslovakia.

Our contact with the members of the Polish Squadron was an extremely happy one. They of course knew that the British personnel had also been helping in their efforts to supply the Underground Army in Poland, and many of them were old friends. However, their willingness to fly to Czechoslovakia after the rupture of relations between the Czechoslovak and Polish Governments was quite surprising. Their anxiousness to do their utmost greatly impressed both the Czech agents and their Conducting Officer.

Our collaboration with the American Airforce was a happy one. They were very keen to fly and to get a clear picture of the work in which they were helping. They were extremely pleased when we could give them fresh information of activities in the Field.

Chapter 8

"Wolfram"

From the moment that the Wolfram party was dropped into the field, it was unfortunate, that first of all they lost one of their most vital men, the W/T operator, Svoboda, who was eventually caught by the Gestapo. As a result of this no direct message was received in London from the party the whole time it served in the field.

Many weeks after the party had been despatched to the field, the news reached London through one of the main organisations that all except Svoboda the W/T operator were safe. This was the only news received from the party until the German capitulation in the Protectorate. In spite of this it had been confirmed by interrogations of the men in the party, that excellent work was done in the field in local organisations, and instructions to partisans in the use of sabotage materials.

Unfortunately, the story of the "Wolfram" party was not obtained from personal interrogation of Captain Otisk, but is a story made up from a written statement prepared by Otisk himself.

Although a standard proforma upon which all party interrogations were based was given to Otisk, it is unfortunate that he did not produce an intelligent narrative. His written story is inadequate, had no continuity, and it was only with difficulty that it could be put together at all.

Svoboda's story was done by personal interrogation at his flat in Prague. Taking the story from Svoboda the impression one was left with was that he was telling the truth. Reading between the lines, it is not difficult to see that he talked a great deal more than he should have done because he was forced to. Against this, he begged it should be taken into account that the torture inflicted upon him, and other agents in the same predicament with the Gestapo, was so terrible that no human being could stand it, and he is not ashamed to say so.

He appears to have confirmed certain beliefs that the Gestapo held on the British set-up, but in spite of his torture, there is no doubt whatsoever that he successfully produced alibis which were eventually responsible for saving the lives of the other men in the "Wolfram" party.

His story reveals the ingenuity of Gestapo interrogation technique, the fanatical contrast in the treatment of agents during interrogations. One day Svoboda was almost beaten to death with taps being turned on down his throat, the next day he was being taken out to lunch by his interrogator and given cigarettes.

This summing up of the Svoboda case is not intended to be a judgment upon him, since at time of writing he awaits trial by Court Martial, when his case will be investigated in detail in a Czech Military Court. When liberated by the Americans Svoboda was a very sick man. In Prague when interrogated by me his nerves were in a very bad state. He was half the weight when previously seen in Italy.

Sabotage materials:	In their initial drop the "Wolfram" party did not carry sabotage materials. It had been arranged with their base in Italy that this material would be dropped to them on their first stores operation.
Documents:	When questioned for documents the party had no trouble at all, but most of the time they lived illegally.
	One of the main reasons for the difficulties experienced by this party on the ground after its drop was that it consisted of six men. Jumping six men through the hole of a Halifax takes a long time.
Suggestions:	In spite of this, Otisk advocates every effort should be made to get all bodies out in one run to ensure that however long the line will be on the ground, all men know approximately their relative positions to each other. This party learnt bitterly from experience, through wide dispersal

after dropping and through the loss of its W/T operator.

Otisk points out that no party should leave for the field with less than two operators and two stations.

Incidents after dropping: After his drop, Otisk was hanging in the tree for twenty minutes. When he eventually reached the ground, he whistled and signalled to his colleagues but got no reply. In the dark he could see nothing and waited until early dawn to get his parachute down off the tree.

After burying it with his striptease he made for a farmhouse a few hundred metres away. Here he learnt from the farmer that a parachutist had dropped near his house and had gone away immediately. From the description he confirmed that this was Svoboda. He also learnt that he was in an area very thickly populated by Germans, so Otisk decided to go deeper into the woods where he searched for a whole day looking for his party. The day's searching brought no results.

At the rendezvous: The next morning, he made for the arranged rendezvous were eventually he found all his colleagues except Svoboda.

The country around was hilly and was covered with thick woods of pine trees some between sixty and ninety feet high. In the valleys there were canyons with small rivers.

Local people: The local people treated the party extremely well, and were very willing to help them with food and information.

Partisans: The partisans repeatedly asked for weapons. He assured them that they would come at the right time.

Local politics: Local politics were strongly democratic, and everyone firmly believed in Beneš. Finding the German oppression unbearable all the civilians were patiently waiting for the day of liberation. German defences in the area were considerable. There were several garrisons and radio location stations.

Sabotage: When contacts were made with the local partisans, the whole party proceeded to give instructions to the partisans in the use of sabotage material, and as a result effective sabotage on the railway between Kromeriz – Zlin – Vestin, was done.

Svoboda was caught on 18 September 1944. His whereabouts being conveyed to the Gestapo by a Czech Quisling.

Bersky was shot on 19 October 1944, by a Gestapo agent.

Chapter 9

Operation Bauxite

This operation involved Captain Paul Hromek. Hromek's mission was to be dropped "Tungston" area and place himself at the disposal of the local commander. Was later instructed through a higher command by Nechansky to proceed to Prague.

Date dropped:	22 March 1945
D.P. location:	At a point 7 kilometres north-east of Velké Mezeřiči in Western Moravia.
Details of drop:	From an operational point of view this flight was a complete success. Hromek and his containers were dropped directly over the reception committee waiting for them. The weather was perfect, there were no clouds, the moon was in its last quarter, there was little wind. Hromek landed 200 metres from the reception lights. He was wearing civilian clothes and a fur lined flying jacket. He was carrying a 45 automatic and a leg bag.
Aircraft load:	The aircraft load consisted of seven containers, five of these for "Platinum", containing two B.2s., two Eurekas, and batteries and M.C.Rs., two containers for Hromek containing one B.2., one Eureka, one hand generator and three six-volt batteries. All of these were dropped successfully over the reception party.
Height:	Dropping from a height of 1,000 feet Hromek was slow in getting out of the plane. He released

his leg bag which dropped perfectly. Its weight was 80 lbs.

Contact with Reception Committee: Five minutes after he dropped, a man ran towards him who said nothing until he was three yards from him. Hromek was ready to shoot and checked the man with the password but did not get any reply. Bearing in mind that the navigator had reported perfect Eureka Rebecca contact and the reception lights on the ground seen, he decided to hold his fire. This man turned out to be a genuine member of the reception committee. A few minutes later Nechansky and Pernicky arrived with the whole of the reception committee. This reception committee had been brought 40 kilometres to do the job.

High spirits and confusion: With the success of this operation the whole of the reception committee were in very high spirits and they were gaily searching the wood for the containers. All were found.

There appeared to be great confusion for the next few moments when the reception committee helped themselves to Hromek's cigarettes, food. Seven men were then attached to Hromek to assist him with his equipment, and walked across country for 14 kilometres. Finding his three batteries too heavy to carry, they dropped them into a lake.

W/T Equipment taken:
One B.2. case type
One Nicholls set
Three batteries
Two 6-volt 40 amp.
One 6-volt 85 amp.
One OP.3. Receiver
One Hand Generator

One English Eureka and spares.

The B.2. gave a good performance throughout, but the Receiver, although very receptive, was too noisy. The Nicholls was also good, using OP.3. receivers which proved much better than M.C.Rs. Hromek divided his W/T equipment at a number of addresses because he could not carry it all with him.

First contact with Italy was on 4 April 1945, transmitted in all 48 messages to Italy and received from Italy 23 messages.

First contact London:	First contact with London was made on the 25 March then for three weeks tried in vain. Made no further contact with London, but was for ten days in April 1945, the only contact with the Protectorate. Hromek maintains the reason for failure to contact London was that London used the "Flint" signal plan Ruzena, instead of the "Jarka" plan.
W/T report:	Hromek's opinion is that the Nicholls set is the best conspiratorial set, but needed more suitable packing for this kind of work. The B.2. vibrator in the power pack was easily fused. The Nicholls set needs different receiver since the M.C.R. is easily broken or parts lost. He recommends the OP.3. for every Eureka operator who has to go a long way to his D.P. and may have to listen to broadcast slogans in the field.
Present location W/T:	Present location of Hromek's W/T material is his flat in Vinohrady, Prague. He has at this address: 1 B.2. 1 Nicholls set 1 Eureka 1 Hand charger

Activities in the Field:	Hromek wishes to pay tribute to the aircraft crew who did a wonderful job flying over the D.P. area. The aircraft approached from the east, turned in over the reception area, dropped containers and Hromek over the D.P. all in the first run. The lights on the ground were excellent.
Field Security:	At a village near the D.P. two days later Hromek questioned the villagers, and found that nobody but the reception committee had any idea that there had been activity that night. The reception committee were apparently very inexperienced in the unpacking of containers, strewing his W/T parts over the ground instead of separating the small containers intact. This behaviour Hromek attributed either to the zeal of the people to get his cigarettes, or to look for weapons.
Hromek grievances:	Hromek lodges a grievance that the Chiefs of the Council of Three were completely ignorant of his uses in W/T and Eureka work, and thinks that he was prevented from contacting this body.
Safe House:	At his first safe house he was confronted with the same old question: when were they going to have weapons. At this house Hromek was given first class food, and found that in the country there was plenty of food. The householders were very frightened of the Gestapo finding Hromek at their house. The security of the reception committee was really excellent. Movement was possible only at night and on foot. Farmers helped him to transport equipment during the day concealed on their carts in hay and potato bags.
Informers:	Hromek was told that in almost every village there were Czech informers.

The condition of the land indicated that all farm people had worked well during the war.

Hromek was convinced that the Czech people became very pro-British when S.O.E. parties appeared in the country to form underground organisations.

Hromek was operating in a very difficult country. It was hilly, much inhabited, with very small distances between the villages.

Local politics: Hromek's impression was strongest local influence was Communist.

The people were very loyal to the Beneš Czech Government.

Hromek lived in the Tunston area, and was, therefore, under the command of Pernicky for the organisation of reception committees.

After a month in the field, he contacted Colonel Josef, Military Representative of the Council of Three, and then proceeded to arrange with him the training of further reception committees.

At this stage Hromek's Prague mission was cancelled.

Summing Up

Hromek had been waiting in England and Italy for nearly two years for an opportunity to be dropped into the Protectorate, and both in Italy and in London showed phenomenal patience. He changed parties and had as many as five different briefings.

When he arrived at the dropping point it appears to be doubtful whether his qualifications were given the best opportunities.

Reading between the lines of his report, and the "Tungston" and "Platinum" reports, it would appear that Hromek was not used to the best of his ability.

Under considerable difficulties he maintained successful vital contact with his W/T, and was for some 10 days, in the vital days of April 1944, the only link with the Protectorate.

Chapter 10

"Manganese"

Names and Ranks:	Cad/Off Vanura S/Mjr Kosina S/Mjr Biros W/T Operator
Mission:	To contact he local organisation in Slovakia and maintain W/T contact with London for passing of intelligence.
Date dropped:	9 June 1944.
Location:	The intended D.P. was at a point 6 kilometres east of Piestany, but the men were actually dropped at Velky Uherec in East Slovakia 80 kilometres from Piestany.
Details of drop:	The party was dropped blind, Vanura jumping with an A-type parachute, Kosina and Biros with X-type chutes.

    The aircraft made two runs, dropping Vanura on the first and Kosina and Biros on the second. All were wearing civilian clothes: Kosina and Biros were carrying no equipment. All wore striptease suits.

    A British crew flew them in a Halifax.

    Over the D.P. at 0100 it began to rain. It was last quarter moon.

    Kosina fell into trees 60 feet high but in just two minutes had cut his way free with only scratches on his nose. He immediately buried his

	parachute. Biros dropped very comfortably in a meadow and at once buried his chute with that of Kosina.
Vanura casualty:	Vanura landed in the garden of a German-owned house, hitting the ground with his head, and was unconscious for fifteen minutes.
W/T equipment taken:	One Simandl complete. Mk.V. Signals plans and crystals. The Simandl was packed in Vanura's A-Type suitcase, one hand generator.
W/T lost	All the W/T material was lost by Vanura, hence no W/T contact was made with London. They were able to inform London of their plight through S.I.S. W/T Station Otto, which they contacted in the Field.
Sehmer:	In August 1944, Major Sehmer's British Mission was dropped into Slovakia carrying a reserve W/T station for the "Manganese" Party.
Relief operation from Italy:	This consisted of a complete B.II. Station Eureka, signal plans and crystals to work to London and Italy. Contact was made with Italy three days later and London after five days.
Kratky:	After a week of good contact with both stations their W/T equipment was taken from them by one Major Kratky and handed to General Golian, commander of the Slovak Rising. Biros and party complained strongly of this, telling Kratky of the "Manganese" London directive but they were ignored.
B.II. performance:	The B.II. was perfect, working well on mains and hand generator.

Activities after dropping:	Kosina and Biros found each other in five minutes after dropping, the distances between them being only 120 yards. Kosina saw Biros dropping. Vanura, who had dropped in the first run, they did not find until a week later.
Insecurity of initial drop:	The nearest village to the drop was 1 kilometre away, Velke Uherte. Later they heard that the villagers had seen them drop and an exaggerated story went round that 15 parachutists had dropped in the area. The Germans were soon out looking for them. Kosina and Biros kept to the woods for two days.
Vanura:	Vanura's story (from Kosina): After the drop Vanura regained consciousness fifteen minutes later, attempted, but failed, to cross a river, so left his equipment in a ditch and set out to look for Kosina and Biros. Failing to find them he asked a local the way to Piestany, the intended D.P., where the party had their safe addresses and set out for them.

Vanura was not accepted at these addresses (the first two) and later Kosina and Biros met with the same result. The house owner just candidly admitted that he was afraid of the Gestapo. The householder, by name Palko, offered them documents and food but would not let them live in his house. |
| Bratislava: | A third safe house would not accept Vanura but accepted Kosina and Biros, putting them in touch with the organisation at Bratislava. This organisation was not very active, the leader having been imprisoned for three years and on release had lost his reason. One Lavicka took Kosina and Biros to Březová, where he linked |

them up with Vanura. Two members of the Bratislava organisation went to Březová to contact "Manganese" Party, take messages and transmit their information to London. Kosina was not sure whether this link was Otto or Zdenka (both S.I.S.).

Failure of relief sortie:
After reunion, all three "Manganese" men moved back to Piestany where they stood by for the next moon period and the pre-arranged emergency W/T stores operation. These relief operations were automatically laid on in Italy before the parties left for the Field. They were fixed to take place at a certain date if the parties did not make W/T contact by that date.

The relief operation did not arrive: the three men went to the D.P. every night until the end of the moon period.

After this they went to Bratislava separately.

Banska Bystrica:
Here they were told by message from London through the Otto contact that the "Manganese" Party would go to Banska Bystrica where they would subordinate themselves to the military organisation there. This was at the end of July 44. The military organisation was then German controlled. Vanura and his party were living as civilians. They produced their London documents without any trouble.

At Bratislava the Germans called them up to join the Slovak forces in Banska Bystrica. Acting on their new briefing from London, they contacted one Major Pollock and then Lieut.-Col. Golian.

At this time Golian had a W/T Station which Kosina believes was working to the East. About

	this time the "Manganese" party heard from Bratislava organisation that their own W/T was in the hands of Gestapo.
Slovak Rising:	In the early part of the month of September the Slovak Rising began.
Golian's command:	Golian took command of the garrisons at Banska Bystrica, Zvolen and Trenchin, including Slovak partisans and parachutists from the East.
Equipment:	Their equipment consisted of only a few armoured cars and a tank.
Sehmer, "Windproof":	Orders came through to "Manganese" telling them to stand by for Major Sehmer and their new W/T equipment.
Davies:	When this party arrived, Davies W/T operator to Sehmer's party called on "Manganese" party at their Banska house, handed over the W/T Station and gave them instructions in the operation of the B.II. set. Golian told Ventura that only his (Golian's) messages were to be sent to British W/T Stations, and that if Biros abused the order, the set would be taken away from him.
Jews:	At the beginning of the rising the enthusiasm for action on the part of the partisans was enormous. Golian's troops set free 4,000 Jews from two camps run by the Germans. These Jews, who appeared to have a lot of money, bought up all the food in the Partisan area and left a very acute shortage among the Slovaks.
Sehmer:	The "Windproof" Party (Major Sehmer) was dropped 30 kilomtres away from their intended D.P. and dropped only 8 kilometres behind the Slovak front line. After some difficulty they convinced the Slovaks they were not Germans.

Sehmer and Golian:	Local leaders then telephoned H.Q. at Banska Bystrica which was expecting the "Windproof" party. Next morning the Sehmer party was driven in great style by car to Banska Bystrica.
Davies and "Manganese":	That evening Sehmer and Davies called on "Manganese" and urged quick contact with Italy with a view to laying on immediate stores' operations to Slovakia. Sehmer's W/T contact was with Force 399 Bari. Sehmer's party first put up at the Hotel and later moved into Golian's H.Q. complete with W/T link to 399.
Russian activity:	Later Sehmer moved from Banska Bystrica because the airfield there was used solely for reception of Russian supplies and a field was under construction at Brezno for the reception of British planes and supplies.
German reinforcements:	In the early days of the rising Golian met with great success overcoming several local German Garrisons until German reinforcements were rushed from Bratislava.
Fall of Bystrica and Brezno:	Sehmer left Banska Bystrica three weeks before it fell. Brezno fell to the Germans five days before Bystrica.
Donovaly:	At the fall of Brystrica, all H.Q. staff, American Mission, and "Manganese" were transferred to Donovaly, to the north of Bystrica.
Last contact:	Here "Manganese" made its last W/T contact with London and Italy. Donovaly was heavily bombed by the Germans and the H.Q. staff fled to the East to join the Russian lines.
Capture of Generals:	Generals Golian and Viest were taken by the Germans at the village of Bukovec on 31 August 1944.

S.O.E. Medical Stores:	Medical stores sent out by S.O.E. from Italy were immensely appreciated by the Slovaks.
The "Manganese" party was enthusiastically received by the Slovak partisans who looked upon their arrival as a sign of tangible help coming from the West.
Russian activity:	During the month of October 1944, Russian planes (five or six each night) dropped supplies of arms to isolated Partisan units. This equipment consisted of anti-tank rifles, Stens and ammunition.
Crude packing of arms:	Kosina saw some of these planes on the ground, and said that Russian packing methods were so crude that most weapons were destroyed. Usual packing was in wooden boxes and thick sacking.
Opinion of Rising:	Kosina's opinion is that had the Slovak Rising been supported with adequate supply of arms and co-ordinated with Allied bombing effort of German garrisons, the Germans could have been defeated. The Germans, he says, always lost their heads when Allied bombers appeared. At the beginning of the Rising the Germans were in the minority, but later two divisions arrived and overran the area.
Kosina a prisoner:	When the Slovak Rising finished, Kosina was taken prisoner (having buried all his equipment) with ten other soldiers when a mountain hut in which they were hiding was surrounded by Wehrmacht troops.
Kosina's successful cover:	All were eventually taken to the Gestapo for questioning. There Kosina cleared himself by passing off as a civilian who had been recruited to join the Slovak forces to take part in this Rising.

"L" tablet:	He was afraid that the Gestapo may have known that he was a parachutist from England, and against this possibility he held his "L" tablet under his tongue, should his story fail with them.
Vanura, Biros shot:	When Biros and Vanura were caught they were interrogated by the Gestapo. No information is available as to the nature of this interrogation, but Kosina learnt from a soldier that both had been taken into the woods and shot. The date was about 31 October 1944, at Bahnicky.
Kosina sees bodies:	In June 1945, a few days prior to this interrogation, Kosina had been to Bahnicky and unearthed the bodies of Vanura and Biros. He had been led to the spot by a local who had been ordered by the Germans to bury the dead after the Rising was over. Both men had been shot through the head. On 3 November 1944, Kosina was released by the Gestapo and went to his home in Lutov in Slovakia. On the way home he was taken by Russian partisans, seeing his Gestapo release pass the Russians were preparing to shoot him. Kosina told them he was a parachutist from England and asked that his father be brought from Lutov to identify him. This was done and Kosina released. Later Kosina organised a small unit of 10 men, performing several acts of ambushing. In this manner Kosina was working when the Russians overran him.
Kosina – Palacek:	He reported to Col. Palacek in May 1945 at Podnin. "Manganese" W/T material is now at Pod-Březnová.

Summing Up

Kosina is the only surviving member of the "Manganese" party.

Meeting with the misfortune of losing their W/T equipment on the first night of their activity in the field, they quickly recovered and made worthy efforts to build up their contacts with London and Italy. A successful relief operation from Italy in August 1944 supplied them with the necessary W/T equipment. From this moment although short lived, they supplied an excellent picture of the Slovak situation at the time of the Slovak Rising.

Constant appeals were made to the West, through this W/T link, for supply of arms. These appeals were not met because of a clear directive from London that Slovakia was a Russian responsibility and no arms to support the rising would be flown from the West. Two operations were laid on from Italy to supply the Slovaks with medical requirements.

Golian's acquisition of the "Manganese" W/T link for his own use was a grave mistake since "Manganese" was silent from that moment and the West was deprived of a vital intelligence link. The "Manganese" party had been subordinated to Golian and were, therefore, not to blame.

In spite of these difficulties the party has acquitted itself well in the field and lived up to the highest ideals of their mission.

Chapter 11

"Sulphur"

Name of Party:	"Sulphur"
Names and ranks:	Lieutenant Horak, Adolf Sergenat Janko, Oldrich
Mission:	Collecting Intelligence and establishing W/T communications in south Bohemia area.
Date dropped:	8 April 1944
Location:	A point 1 kilometre south-south-east of Vsetaty.
Details of drop:	"Sulphur" Party has been missing since day of operation.
Only Clue:	From the day that the "Sulphur" Party was dropped the only available clue as to what happened to these two men is obtained from an interrogation of one Matras, Joseph who was a friend of Janko's before the war. They were both in France before the war and met in Paris in 1936. Janko stayed in France but Matras returned to Praha in 1938. In 1941, Matras heard that Janko had joined the Czech Army in France. In June 1944 Matras met Janko in the Café Tlapah in Praha, where they talked. Janko told Matras that he had been dropped by parachute from England, but did not say anything else of his activity. Matras got him food and cigarettes.

In October Janko said "Goodbye" to Matras but did not say where he was going.

No other news of the "Sulphur" party has come to light from the Field, and no S.O.E. agent saw the "Sulphur" men in the Field.

When the Gestapo took Trpik, Cikan and Hanina ("Glucinium") to the Pankrác prison in Prague they told Trpik that Horak and Janko had been caught in Prague.

Chapter 12

"Chalk"

Names and Ranks: Captain Bednarik, Bohumil
Sergeant Nedelka, Frantisek
Warrant Officer Kunkl, Joseph
Warrant Officer Hauptvogel, Vladimir

Mission: To establish contact with the underground organisation in Bohemia and to make contact with London by W/T.

Details: The "Chalk" Party was captured by the Gestapo on or about 9 April 1944, almost immediately after being dropped.

From this moment they collaborated with the Gestapo in every way, transmitting to London under Gestapo orders, and on at least one occasion setting up Eureka in a field on the night of British operations to the Protectorate.

Major Nechansky states that during their captivity "Chalk" Party worked as collaborators with a group of Russian parachutists who were also taken by the Gestapo. Because of this the Russian N.K.V.D. suddenly arrested Bednarik, Nedelka and Kunkl in their Praha flat in May 1945, taking them without reference to Czech Chiefs of Staff to the N.K.V.D. H.Q. at Mor. Ostrava. They were released one month later and immediately imprisoned by the Czech military in Praha where they await trial by Court Martial. They were not released for interrogation.

W/O Hauptvogel was shot by the Gestapo when he attempted escape.

No other information is available about this party.

Chapter 13

"Glucinium"

Name and Ranks:	Lieutenant Leparik Warrant Officer Trpik, Frantisek S/M Hanina, Ludwig Warrant Officer Cikan, Joseph
Mission:	Intelligence from the Field to London covering location of enemy troops movements, etc.
Date dropped:	4 July 1944
Location:	Intended D.P. was at Tabor, but the Party actually landed at a appoint 18 kilometres north of Ceske-Budejovice in South Bohemia.
Details of drop:	Party was dropped blind into southern Bohemia. They were flown in a Halifax with a Canadian crew in perfect weather and quarter moon.
Parachutes:	Leparik and Trpik jumped with A-type parachutes, Hanina and Cikan with X-type chutes, carrying rucksacks on the chest. The men jumped from 800 feet. When Leparik went through the hole the suitcase became detached from his parachute and was five hours later found in pieces on a road, with its contents and W/T equipment damaged beyond repair. All four men fell into trees but were not injured. Cikan was twenty minutes up the tree but the others got down in under 10 minutes. All their parachutes were caught in the trees and for nearly

nine hours they struggled to get them down. They gave up in the end, leaving all the chutes in the trees. The suitcase attached to Trpik's A-type chute was suspended with the chute up a tree at approx. 70 feet. This they had to leave as well, as dawn was approaching. A passing cyclist was a cue for the party to get away.

W/T materials: The "Glucinium" Party took with them one Mk.5 receiver, one Simandl, one Mk.15 Transreceiver, spare parts and signal plans. Trpik carried the signal plan on his person. Leparik carried the Mk.5 power pack and Mk.15 in his suitcase and A-Type chute. He states that when his chute opened, he looked up and saw no bag.

Since all this equipment was beyond repair, no W/T contact was made with London or Italy.

Activities in the Field: Failing after nine hours to get their parachutes and suitcases off the trees, efforts which were assisted by nearby villagers, the "Glucinium" Party moved off.

It must be recorded that this party had no materials for breaking or sawing down trees. Trpik says he asked the pilot not to drop them in the woods at any cost.

Buried equipment: At a distance of two kilometres away from their D.P. they buried all their broken W/T equipment.

That night they set off for their first safe address at Tyn on the Vltava. (In their first day they passed off as civilians).

They called on a certain Svoboda, a basket-maker, who refused to help them and later told the Czech Gendarmerie about them. While hiding in woods, Trpik was surprised by a Czech policeman who captured him. He was taken to a local house where he was told that Leparik had called to pay his respects to the daughter. Trpik states that Leparik saw him being taken and warned him off by loud talking.

Leparik disappears: It worked and Leparik made off to hide in some tall wheat. The Czech gendarme proved to be a sympathiser and invented a yarn to cover Trpik and let him go. Trpik returned at once to the hide-out where Cikan and Hanina were waiting. Here they waited for the return of Leparik, who did not arrive.

Burying Leparik's materials the three men crossed the Vltava at Bernartice.

Safe addresses: They had three safe addresses given to them from London. They learned from a local woodman that the families of all three houses were dead. Later this woodman brought them food into the woods where they stayed the night.

Disagreement: The remaining three men of "Glucinium" Party could not agree on a plan of action. They arrived at the village of Pezdelane where they contacted a man named Horky whom Hanina said he knew. By this time "Glucinium" had no safe address left to which to go. Nobody in this village was prepared to help them and Horky did not arrive at the arranged meeting.

Gestapo alarm: At the village of Zkore an alarm was sent up to the whole area that three parachutists were at large. All the villagers were eyeing them suspiciously so they moved to Vladisky. Here they stayed with a sympathetic farmer for three nights. This farmer told them about the alarm and gave them a safe house at Tabor.

Hanina and Cikan now said they wanted to stay in Bohemia: Trpik was for going to Slovakia and the Russian lines. The latter plan was agreed to.

Trpik betrayed: At Třebič Trpik tried to get a pair of new shoes for Cikan from someone he knew working at the Bata factory. He went to meet this man and on returning to a pre-arranged spot he found that Cikan and Hanina had disappeared. Enquiring of women working in the fields, he was told that they had been seen heading S.E.

Interrogators Note: At this point in the interrogation of Trpik, Hanina and Cikan they were all three picked up in my company by a guard of the Chiefs of Staff H.Q. and taken to prison in Prague to await trial by court martial. They were not released for the interrogation to finish. The rest of the story is taken from a translation of their individual stories.

Trpik alone: After a long wait he decided to move on, sleeping that night on a haystack. His destination was Brno. On the road he was asked by a Czech gendarme for his Arbeitsbuch. He hadn't one but produced his Občanská legitimace, which did not satisfy the gendarme who took him to the Station.

On the way Trpik asked the gendarme if his superior officer was a Czech, but got an evasive answer. At the station Trpik soon saw that he was trapped: his pistol was inaccessible and armed policemen were at the only exit.

Trpik caught: Seeing that he could not escape he told them that he was a parachutist and that they must give him back his "L" tablet before the Gestapo arrived. The gendarmes told him that they did not believe his story and called in the Gestapo, who took him to Julhava and then to Brno.

On the way Trpik prepared a story in his mind and told them his name was Tichy. At Brno the Gestapo told him that they had caught Laparik and that he would see him later. He refused to describe Cikan and Hanina thinking that Laparik might have already described them.

Czech informers: He discovered, however, that the people of Ruzove had already given a description of Cikan and Hanina. The Gestapo showed Trpik a list of names and details of S.T.S. 46 and other names in the British S.O.E. set-up, also a picture of S.I.S. leader.

The Gestapo also had a picture of Bogataj, leader of "Carbon", when he was a cadet in Military College. Then in came a tall, slim official who asked him "What's old Palocok doing. He's one of the clever ones in London." Trpik says that from this moment he gave up all hope of suicide.

Return to D.P: That night the Gestapo took Trpik to his D.P. to look for his equipment but returned without finding it. Back at Brno he was again questioned and told the Gestapo the calibre of the pistols carried by Cikan and Hanina.

When asked for his safe address Trpik said Leparik only knew them.

Bodnarik: Trpik was brought into Praha in August 1944, where he met Bodnarik of "Chalk" Party. The Gestapo had previously had Bodnarik mixed up with Leparik, and had their names on the wrong photographs.

Cikan and Hanina: Cikan and Hanina were soon caught and when brought before Trpik they asked him what he had said to the Gestapo. Trpik was advised by Cikan

	to tell the Gestapo everything, indicating that he, Cikan, had given them the whole story.
Quisling Frank:	Later Minister K.H. Frank (Sudeten German Quisling leader) spoke to all three men, and asked Hanina if he would speak on the radio. Hanina replied that he was a very bad speaker. Cikan in reply to the same question gave a negative answer.
Leparik:	Leparik was caught in September 1944, and told the three of them that he had lost them when he had hidden after the Svoboda house incident.
Trpik accuses Leparik:	Trpik accused Leparik of not waiting to hear the result of the incident and making off. Leparik declared that he had visited all the safe addresses and had joined a partisan group until he got word that Horak of "Sulphur" Party was ill in Prague.
Leparik's flimsy story:	In Prague looking for Horak, Leparik states he had a fight with someone in the passage of the Vaclaska Namasti (Prague's most famous street) and was caught by the Gestapo. Bednarik told Trpik that [illegible] was in Hradic hospital very ill after his suicide attempt and was being watched.
Horak and Hanko:	The Gestapo told "Glucinium" Party that they had caught Horak and Janko of "Sulphur" Party. Later it was proved to the "Glucinium" boys that all their answers to Gestapo interrogations were different. Trpik declared that the Gestapo were forcing Bednarik ("Chalk") to transmit to London on his W/T link.
Escape attempt:	They all planned an escape attempt and tried it in April but the attempt was stopped by the Gestapo. They were then separated, Trpik was

	taken to Pankrac prison in Prague where he was released by the people of the city when the rising began on 5 May 1945.
Cikan alone:	Up to the time when he lost touch with Trpik at Borovany near Třebič, Cikan's story confirms Trpik's. Cikan and Hanina were caught on 5 August 1944. Two civilians on bicycles approached them on a country road and when they were abreast jumped off and held up Cikan and Hanina at pistol point. Within a few minutes these men were joined by four others, all armed.
Captured:	Cikan and Hanina were put on to a lorry flat on their faces, arms extended, and taken to Gestapo H.Q. at Brno.
Prague:	A week later they were both taken to Pankrac prison in Prague. Quisling Frank asked Cikan what he thought of conditions in Bohemia. Cikan replied that he had expected them to be much worse.

When offered a chance to collaborate Cikan turned it down. Cikan also confirms that Bednarik was forced to transmit to England.

After this Cikan had nothing to add until he was released from prison in Prague during the rising. |
| Hanina alone: | Hanina reports that all the safe addresses given to "Glucinium" party in London were two years out of date, and they were all in the hands of the Gestapo.

Hanina's story confirms Cikan's up to the time they separated from Trpik. |
| Janc and Kubcik: | At Brno Hanina was shown photographs of Janc and Kubcik, and was told they had committed suicide. |

	Hanina was also taken to Prague prison. From there to Jenerahu prison, where he found Bednarik, Kunzel, Nedelka of "Chalk" party, and Trpik.
"Sulphur":	Here Hanina says he found that Horak and Janko had been collaborating with the Gestapo, and that it was Horak's talking which had led to the capture of Bednarik's party.
Nedelka:	Once a week Nedelka was taken to Benesov and forced to contact London on W/T, and one-night Bednarik and Kunzel.
Forced Eureka contact:	Went out with the Gestapo and set up Eureka in a Field.
Leparik:	Leparik was now collaborating effectively, the Gestapo telling Hanina and Cikan that he was sensible and clever and would soon be free in Prague. One day Leparik arrived drunk at the prison with a large party of drunken Gestapo officers. Hanina was also released in the Prague rising.
Hanina accuses Trpik:	In the Czech interrogation carried out at the Chiefs of Staff H.Q. in Prague, Hanina accused Trpik of several betrayals of safe addresses and routes, to the Gestapo, and maintains that they were caught because Trpik told the Gestapo of a route they would eventually take to find a safe address.

Summing Up

The "Glucinium" Party failed in the Field in every sense of the word. Losing their equipment on the night of the operation they subsequently made no attempt to contact London through established underground organisations.

They were outrageously careless in the Field in matters of security. Hanina gave a farmer 1000 rounds and his 32 pistol for housing himself and Cikan for four nights.

There can be little doubt that this party saved its own skin by talking to the Gestapo and eventually they accuse each other of betrayal of their own safe addresses, etc. Trpik's story of his capture is so thin that it would appear he almost walked into the trap consciously.

Their individual stories are so full of contradictions that it is impossible to believe one or the other. They were all three, Cikan, Hanina and Trpik, arrested in Prague in June 1945, and at time of writing this report, they await court martial trial by the Czech Military Court in Prague.

This report and summing up is not intended to be a final word on the honour or loyalty of these men since their case has yet to be fully investigated and proved by Czech Military Court.

It is a report based on their own words in personal interrogation and their own written statements.

Chapter 14

"Clay"

Names and Ranks: Captain Bartos, Antonin
Lieutenant Sikola, Costmir (W/T Op.)
Lieutenant Stokman

Mission: Intelligence and communications from the Field.

Date to be dropped: 12 April 1944.

Location: Successfully dropped to intended dropping point at Priluky, in Moravia.

Details of Drop: The "Clay" Party was dropped into the Field blind, at a point Zasova, 10 kilometres south of Priluky. The aircraft, a Halifax, was flown by a Canadian crew.

Also flying on this night was the "Carbon" Party. They flew in the last quarter moon in good weather but with slight mist.

Bartos and Sikola jumped with A-type parachutes, Stokman with X-type. They all wore striptease and civilian clothes. Bartos and Sikola jumped with rucksacks on the chest, and were despatched with their A-type chutes by Captain Hrubec, who flew with the parties for this purpose. The men jumped from 2,000 feet owing to the height of the hills being 1,000 feet.

Using the A-types, Bartos and Sikola jumped successfully. The whole party was dropped in one run and landed comfortably in a field with approximately 150 yards between each man.

Within twenty minutes all three were together with equipment o.k. and no casualties. The nearest village was two kilometres away.

The Party had no time to give the aircraft an o.k. signal with their torches.

W/T Equipment taken: Simandl, with Mk.5 receiver.
1 M.R. 5 Transreceiver and spares.

First Contact: The Simandl was carried in Bartos' A-Type. Sikola carried the Mk.5 receiver and the MR. 5. All equipment landed undamaged.

First contact with London was made a fortnight later, on the Simandl with the Mark 5 reception.

In the interests of security, and owing to the great power of the Simandl transmitter, they decided to bury it and work with Mk.5 receiver.

Waterproofing W/T: In order to lighten their weight after dropping, Bartos had waterproofed the Mk.5 transreceiver and buried it in a stream. When they went back to it they took it out and started a successful transmission with it.

For one year the Mk.5 gave consistent and excellent performance to London until April 1945, when the electricity was cut and they had no power to work it. In this time Sikola encoded 750 telegrams to London and decoded 200 telegrams from London. September 1944, was the peak month when the "Clay" party sent 180 telegrams to London.

The longest gap in the transmission of messages was only ten days. On the 11th April 1945, in Zlin, Bartos heard that the Gestapo were looking for them. This was the last contact with London. Bartos and Sikola give all the W/T equipment a first-class report. This equipment, i.e., the Mk 5 receiver and the Simandl, are at Brno. The Mk 5 transmitter is lost.

Documents: Most of the time "Clay" party was in the Field its members lived illegally, but on those occasions when their documents were checked they had no difficulties.

Activities on arrival: The three men of the "Clay" party quickly recovered themselves after the drop. After dividing their equipment and burying that not required immediately, they at once got away from their D.P. following a compass bearing in the direction of Priluky. Snow was thick on the ground. They made their march through the woods, and eventually arrived at their first safe address at Bystrica P. Hostynon.

Bartos went into the village to call at the house while Sikola and Stokman waited outside. At the house Bartos met the wife of the household who would not believe his story that he was a parachutist from London. Bartos, however, became threatening and said he would remain in her house till she fetched her husband. Meanwhile Bartos decided to go back for Sikola and Stokman. When they returned to the house the husband was at home.

At first he also was reluctant to believe Bartos' story. However, in the end he was convinced and decided to hide the party. Nevertheless, there was considerable doubt in the man's mind, so Bartos proposed that he should go into the woods to see for himself where the parachutes were hidden.

Before the husband could do this however, news was spreading through the village that the local Czech police had found them and had handed them over to the Gestapo. This news definitely cleared the last element of doubt from the man's mind. This man's address had been given to Bartos from somebody in the Czech Brigade in London. His name was Prohazka and he was well known as an anti-Nazi. Nevertheless, his only contribution to Bartos in his work was to hide the party.

First plans: In this area no underground organisation existed, so in May 1944 Bartos began to organise an underground movement.

Three locals were recruited for their first meeting. One Kucora, a policeman, Zichacok, a policeman, and one Philip. The meeting took place in Kucora's house. Bartos' plan was to build an organisation on the Beaulieu methods, so he arranged that each of the six men should recruit three men apiece and so build an organisation like this until it was large enough to cover Eastern Moravia.

Eventually Bartos' organisation covered Hranice, Holosovo, Velké Mezerice, Vsetin, where in each of these districts there were some thirty men collecting intelligence for Bartos, head of the organisation.

Complete organisation: By 28 May 1944, this large network was collecting intelligence which was being transmitted to London. Many of the recruited men were previously serving officers and it was their ardent desire for active warfare that led them to demand repeatedly from Bartos deliveries of arms.

Request for arms: Although Bartos had been despatched to the Field solely to build up an intelligence organisation he relented and despatched news of these requests for arms to London.

London orders:	In reply from London, he received a "rocket" and was told that he must stick to his intelligence contacts and not attempt to build up a military organisation.
	Bartos was fortunate in having in his organisation loyal Czechs who were now gendarmes and police in the area. Difficulties of documents and passes did not exist. Bartos was always advised when there was to be a road control or an inspection and was therefore able to avoid them.
	In spite of London's decision that he should stick to intelligence work, Bartos anticipated still more demands from his men for arms and proceeded to build up his military organisation.
Russian advance:	As the Russian advance moved forward in Slovakia Czech headquarters, London, asked Bartos for details of his military organisation.
	Bartos replied that he had built up a force to cover an area to receive arms for 3,000 men. After this, plans for the military organisations went forward.
Military leaders:	One Colonel Rakovcik was brought by one of Bartos' trusted agents to take over command of the underground movement with one Colonel Vitek as second in command.
London approval:	Bartos sent this news to London who asked him to organise the reception of stores. All the plans were made and passwords arranged and by the appointed time this underground army was standing by.
	After all this perfect organisation and first-class planning, Bartos' great organisation got no stores or equipment.

Bartos' worst moments:	He says that this was the worst time in the whole period of his work in the Field, because over and over again he was obliged to tell his leaders that his underground army had to wait and keep on waiting.
Gestapo movements:	At this time the Gestapo was organising new formations against the development of reception committees and parachutists. After capturing a former Prerova agent belonging to the organisation the Gestapo in December 1944, penetrated the organisation.
A double agent:	This agent, to save his own neck, went over to work for the Gestapo. This man managed to reach Bartos through one of his leaders, and this confidant of the Gestapo proceeded to tell Bartos that he had an organisation in West Moravia, with 300 L.M.G.s.
The Zlin organisation:	Previously Bartos had been warned by his Zlin agents that this man had been having trouble in Zlin with an organisation he had been building up there.
Bartos' suspicions:	In this first meeting Bartos told this double agent to carry out certain orders, but was disobeyed. In his second meeting with Bartos the latter's suspicions were confirmed and after his meeting was over Bartos gave his Zlin agents orders to shoot the Gestapo agent as soon as possible. This man was eventually shot by partisans. Other cases of double agents were encountered by Bartos, and on one occasion the Czech news from England broadcast a message to the effect that "Frantisek Schmidt was a Gestapo agent and should be shot on sight."

Change of headquarters:	On 29 December, Bartos moved his headquarters from Central Moravia to the village of Tvrdonice near Hodinin in South Moravia.
Transmissions were again made to London on the 7 January 1945, and connections were again made with the organisation still in the north east.
Courier difficulties:	This was done by a constant stream of agents working on a courier system. Sometimes messages took a week to reach Bartos at his new headquarters. Whenever anything went wrong with the security of a dropping point Bartos at once changed it and transmitted new passwords to London.
Bartos' leader in Zlin sent a message saying that his work for the underground movement was so much that he felt he was being suspected by the Gestapo, and he decided to disappear and live illegally.
Capture of Zlin leader:	Before doing this the Zlin leader went home to his wife where officers of the Gestapo were waiting for him. He was caught and the next day the Gestapo also picked up the couriers between Zlin and Bartos.
Later, five Gestapo men accompanied one of these couriers to Bartos' headquarters at Tvrdonice. Arriving at the house they watched the courier enter the house and contact Bartos, who was having supper.
At the table there were five men having supper, and since the numbers were equal the Gestapo decided to lie low for a few hours.
Bartos cornered:	In the morning the Gestapo men were accompanied by 30 S.S. men. At 06.00 hours, when it was still dark the woman of the house told Bartos that the house was surrounded.

Before waiting for the dawn Bartos decided to run for it, and jumped out of the ground floor window, his 38 automatic with dum-dum bullets in his hand. When he was fifteen yards from the house the S.S. men opened up with machine guns.

The fire power was so tremendous that Bartos flung himself to the ground, at the same time badly injuring his right hand as he hit the ground on the very hard ice. As he went through the window Bartos was firing furiously and learnt later that he had succeeded in killing three Gestapo men.

Sikola and Stokman had been living separately in the next village. Now all the villagers were turning out to see what the shooting was all about.

They move on: During the next day, the "Clay" party stayed under cover and at night moved on to Prušánky. Here they reported the story to London by W/T and again contacted the rest of their organisation.

Again, Bartos changed dropping points and passwords, and found a new leader for the Zlin organisation. This new Zlin leader lasted a fortnight before he was caught by the Gestapo. Members of the Zlin organisation asked the "Clay" party to go to Zlin where they arrived by car on Good Friday. The next day their guide and driver were both picked up by the Gestapo.

At this stage Bartos' great organisation was crumbling and being picked up by the Gestapo in many parts of the country.

Last contact with London: It was in Zlin that they made their last contact with London on Easter Saturday, 1945, with the M.R.5 trans-receiver.

Moving again to south Moravia, they failed to make any further contact with London because the electric power for the whole district of Brno was cut off, and the W/T operator had no hand-charging equipment.

His silence: During the vital months when operations to Moravia reached a peak of activity Bartos was silent and was not able to avail himself of these operations. Nevertheless, Bartos maintains that he heard the B.B.C. slogans and that his reception committees were standing by.

Several attempts were made to deliver special equipment to Bartos when he was standing by near Hodonin.

Bartos who lived nearly a whole year in hiding, must be complimented on his devotion to duty, especially when one bears in mind that on one occasion, he lived only 2 kilometres from his pre-war girlfriend and his family. Bartos stuck religiously to his Beaulieu training and avoided women for a whole year.

Russians: The "Clay" party waited at Prušánky until the Russians overran them, and on 14 April, Bartos and his party came out into the open and headed for Kosice, where they reported to Colonel Palceck.

Early impressions: When they arrived in the Field on the night of their operation, one of the first impressions they had was that restrictions on Moravia were not strictly enforced. He confirms that conditions were very much better than they had been led to believe. At least on the food question and the general movements of the people.

	He found the Narodni Viber very unreliable so he did not disclose himself to them, and avoided them the whole time.
Attitude of the Czechs:	All members of the vast organisation built up by Bartos gave him all help and encouragement and always regarded the party as the "voice from the West". In spite of the readiness of the Czechs to co-operate in his work Bartos chose his agents very carefully.
Political tendencies:	Beneš for President again was the thought uppermost in the minds of the people. The people wanted three political parties in the country, Communist, Labour and Conservative. Bartos thought the Labour party was the strongest. He transmitted all this intelligence to London.
Reception Committees:	At each dropping point the Reception Committees were made up of thirty men, and in all there were over three hundred people trained to do Reception work by the "Clay" party. In accordance with his briefing from London to stick to intelligence work Bartos did not attempt any sabotage.

Summing Up

The work of the "Clay" party is outstanding. Bartos and W/T operator made what is probably the finest contribution as an intelligence link between the Protectorate and England. This intelligence was of the greatest interest and value to the Czech and British Governments in London.

The fact that 750 messages were sent to London, and over 200 received from London, and in one peak month 180 messages were transmitted, indicating the exceptional qualities of Bartos as an organiser and Sikola as a W/T operator and Stokman as a decoder and encoder.

The skill and great organising genius that Bartos showed in successfully building up a large underground organisation deserves the very highest praise.

Chapter 15

"Carbon"

Names and Ranks:	Major Bogataj, Frantisek Lieutenant Sperl, Jaroslav, W/T Op. Lieutenant Kobzik, Frantisek Lieutenant Vanc, Joseph
Mission:	Collecting intelligence in the Field and organisation of Reception Committees.
Date dropped	13 April 1944
Location:	Vacenovic in south-east Moravia
Details of W/T:	Only W/T equipment to survive the initial drop was one Eureka. First contact with London giving news of W/T plights of "Carbon" was through "Clay" party. On 28 January 1945, contact was made with London on a set made by a local radio expert at Kunovice. From this time "Carbon" maintained regular contact, eventually transmitting 213 telegrams.
Details of drop:	Bogataj and his party dropped into trees at the edge of a large wood, their parachutes being clearly seen from a nearby village. Bogataj was suspended in the trees for some time and lost his party. When he did drop to the ground, he searched for his party for two hours without success. Twenty-four hours later he still had not found them, and

carrying his Eureka and personal equipment he made for the pre-arranged rendezvous, which he reached on the second night.

News reached him that the dropping point had been surrounded by S.S. police and gendarmerie, and a big search was going on for his party.

All the boys were well away in time, however, but did not appear at the rendezvous.

First contact organisation: After waiting for twenty-four hours there, Bogataj visited a man named Hronik, who although not a safe address given to him in London, helped him.

He was put into touch with a local school teacher named Straka, a member of an underground organisation, and Bogataj asked him to start a search for his missing party.

In the first week of his arrival, Bogataj heard the local radio station announcer asking the people in the area to surrender the parachutists in the district. About ten times a day the villagers were warned against helping the "Carbon" party.

Later Bogataj contacted one Captain Francovi, and asked him to go to one area underground leader named Sterba and report his presence. Just in time Bogataj discovered that Francovi had betrayed him to the Gestapo, and got away, but Hronik, who sheltered Bogataj for one night, was caught at the end of April.

News of Sperl: Straka brought the news that one Mrs Hrabalove was sheltering Sperl at her house in Vesky. Bogatak established immediate contact with him. Sperl reported that he had buried all his W/T equipment where he had dropped but had not returned to it since the whole area was being watched and searched by large numbers of S.S. men.

Second attempt betrayal:

Bogataj then proceeded to search for a party that could give London information of his plight. Straka told him of a W/T station at Brno saying that he would arrange a contact.

He produced one Rysanek, who offered to act as courier to Brno, saying that he would want the message in clear and also a photograph of Bogataj for getting identity documents etc. Confirming Bogataj's suspicions about this man, the London Czech B.B.C. news at about this time announced that Rysanek was a traitor and should be shot at sight.

Later Bogataj heard that two injured parachutists were sheltering at a safe address in Rutice, near Bojkovice. The house was surrounded and attacked by the Gestapo. The men were Vanc and Kobjik of Bogataj's party.

Cornered, with no chance of escape, Kobzik first shot Vanc, then himself. Vanc's pistol was found fully loaded. Straka and Bogataj tried to search for their W/T but without success.

Bogataj finds Bartos:

In September 1944, Bogataj contacted Bartos, of "Clay" party in Moravia, asking him to ask London to send new W/T equipment to him at once. London promised him his stores, but although Bogataj waited with his Eureka nine times over the chosen dropping point he received nothing.

Bogataj then asked Bartos if he could lend him his second reserve W/T station until he (Bogataj) got his material from Italy. This Bartos would not do. Bogataj, not to be defeated, arranged with a radio expert in Kunovice, one Mr Kuchar, for one W/T set to be made with local materials.

W/T traffic:	This was done and at last "Carbon" party contacted London on its own signals plan on 28 January 1945.
	In spite of a long silence until this date, Bogataj and Sperl had been working and planning their future operations very carefully. Since he had been dropped Bogataj had organised and trained Reception Committees for twenty-three D.P.s. He now gave London the names of his sub-leaders, and locations of his D.P.s on his W/T.
Third betrayal:	With the advances of the Russians, Bogataj's reception parties became impatient and the situation tense. The woman who housed Sperl was then caught by the Gestapo and gave away the name of six of Bogataj's sub-leaders, including Straka and one Vitek.
Straka:	Straka, a key man in the organisation, committed suicide before the Gestapo could work on him, and was secretly buried by the Gestapo. Another of the six men attempted suicide by cutting his veins but was caught doing so by the Gestapo.
	Towards the middle of April 1945, the Germans cut all electric power in Brno and S. Moravia, putting an end to Bogataj's transmissions to London.
Successful operations:	In April, operations to fly stores, arms and other equipment were considerably stepped up to the "Carbon" area, and although at this time no W/T contact was possible with Bogataj, his good work in the previous months resulted in many successful operations.
	By this time, however, it was too late, as the Germans, in the face of the Russian advance,

had strengthened all their garrisons and prepared special anti-parachutist measures.

Gestapo got stores: In many operations the Germans were themselves looking for stores dropped to "Carbon" and large amounts of the equipment flown from Italy fell into the hands of the Gestapo.

The "Carbon" party was particularly unfortunate at the hands of Czech informers, who searched for the buried equipment and told the Gestapo.

German repression had made people afraid to help Bogataj in his work.

Peak operations: Bogataj states that he received only eight stores operations, three of them being successful. Of the five other operations the Gestapo got most of the material.

The quantities of arms received were not sufficient to commence a rising of the people.

Successful sabotage: Nevertheless, it was used by the parties very successfully in sabotage operations, the most successful of which were:

1. Attack on airport at Kunovice.
2. Destruction of mine dump depot.
3. several attacks on trains carrying Hungarian troops.
4. Railways, telephone exchanges.
5. One of Bogataj's groups, under the leadership of one Konecny, liberated Popovace and surrounding villages before the arrival of the Russian troops.

Later this party assisted the Russians to liberate Uh. Hradiště.

In this sub-unit they suffered seven dead and nine injured.

Many of Bogataj's couriers went through the German lines to give intelligence to the advancing Russians.

As the Russian advance got very near, all groups of the underground organisation openly took up the fight, although not sufficiently armed.

Summing Up

The contribution to the Czechoslovak Resistance Movement made by the "Carbon" Party is outstanding.

In spite of almost complete lack of help from the West until practically the last moment, Bogataj and his men did great work in the Field organising twenty-three dropping points and Reception Committees. They collected vital intelligence on the situation in East and South East Moravia and successfully transmitted this to London.

All the time they lived under great difficulties, dodging the Gestapo and living in hiding most of the time.

It was Bogataj's most unpleasant duty to promise weapons to his Reception Committees and repeatedly explain away their non-arrival. Eventually the step-up of the "Carbon" stores operations arrived when the Germans had policed almost every kilometre in Moravia in the face of the Russian advance. In spite of this, most effective sabotage was carried out by Bogataj's organisation behind the German lines on communications, airfields, mine dumps, and movement of troops.

Lieutenants Vanc and Kobzik lost their lives, committing suicide when cornered by the Gestapo. Sperl's performance as a W/T operator was exceptional and deserves the highest credit.

Bogataj was a great leader who showed great genius in his organising ability.

Chapter 16

"Tungsten" (S.I.S.)

This this is included in this account, as, although it is officially an S.I.S. Party, the work it did was 100% S.O.E.

Names:	[Redacted]
Mission:	To establish pick-up for courier planes and organise reception of persons and materials.
Date dropped:	21 December 1944, at 22.20 hours.
Location:	The intended D.P. was W of Policka in N.W. Moravia but the party was actually dropped three miles south of Kolin in Bohemia, 35 miles from the intended D.P.
W/T:	The "Tungsten" Party was briefed as in above mission and ordered to place itself at the disposal of the Council of Three taking Eureka but no W/T equipment.
Details of drop:	The "Tungsten" Party was to be dropped blind at the point west of Policka. They wore strip-tease suits over civilian clothes.

There was a slight mist over the ground and 1st quarter moon, and both men were dropped at 1200 feet.

Both men jumped with the special type leg bag i.e. a bag considerably larger than the leg bag strapped to the leg, which has a small parachute of its own but is attached to the jumper's harness by a 12-foot rope.

[Redacted] released his bag perfectly and reached the ground without damage. [Redacted] however, lost his bag as soon as he pulled the leg bag parachute cord. The bag fell straight to the ground from 1000 feet.

In spite of this, [Redacted]'s leg bag was found, three hundred yards away and the contents undamaged. Reasons given for this mishap, is careless tying of suspension rope to parachute harness.

The Eureka was carried in [Redacted]'s bag. All their materials were completely packed in rucksacks on being taken out of the leg bags, leaving the party ready to move at once.

In the Field: In spite of being dropped 35 miles away from the D.P. at Policka, the "Tungsten" party dropped comfortably in a meadow, and were not seen or heard by anybody.

They were only 100 yards away from each other and contacted each other at once. After a search of 1½ hours they found [Redacted]'s leg bag, then put all their material on top of a hay stack after putting the parachute and striptease in the leg bag.

They had absolutely no idea where they were and commenced walking towards a village 1 kilometre away. They were now carrying the Eureka and all their personal equipment, Sten guns and pistols. [Redacted] also carried crystals for S.I.S. Party Zdenka.

Continuing their march in a S.E. direction, walking only through woods and fields, they later discovered they were near Kutna Hora. They remained all day in the wood, where a gamekeeper saw them and made off quickly.

Neither knew this part of the country, so [Redacted] decided to go into the village: there he asked a woman how to get to a certain town by train. The answer gave him the clue he needed.

Back in the woods he planned his route through the fields and woods to Studnice near Novo Mesto. For eight days and nights they were exposed to cold with snow all the way. During the day they stayed in the woods in any kind of hiding. Although they did not have enough food, they did not contact any Czechs to get any.

Throughout the march they had only the following foods:

1. 1 packet each 24 hr rations.
2. 1 tin of sweets each.
3. 1 tin of special rations (concentrated foods).
4. 1 tin of chocolate cocoa, which they made by boiling snow.

On these foods they existed for eight days. Their rucksacks weighed 50 lbs each. Eventually they arrived at their first safe address, one Cyril Musil owner of a ski pension at Studnice. [Redacted] was by this time completely out and at the end of his resistance.

Condition: For a fortnight both could hardly walk because their feet and legs were so swollen. [Redacted] pays great tribute to the care and hospitality his host showed them. During this painful fortnight neither [Redacted] could have run for it had the Gestapo been after them.

First contact While recovering [Redacted] contacted one Colonel Richard, Military Deputy of the Council of Three also Siroky of Zdonka, who sent word to London with news of "Tungsten" plight.

[Redacted] were hidden in a top room of Cyril Musil's house, their presence known only to his family but not to the ski visitors. They were given excellent food.

Request for arms

The local underground organisers were begging [Redacted] for arms to equip Reception Committees. [Redacted]'s job of organising reception of courier planes was made impossible by deep snow 6 feet deep. [Redacted] then offered to organise reception parties in reception of stores, and gave Colonel Richard a picture of the Italian stores set-up.

The Council of Three were heads of the vast Moravian underground organisation. [Redacted] reports that the security of this organisation was perfect. Russian organisations of partisans gave the impression of not being so security-minded. [Redacted] did not contact Russian parachutists.

All the members of the Moravian organisation were desperately anxious to rise against the Germans but could do nothing without weapons. [Redacted] reported this through his Zdonka link. German troops and civilians gave "Tungsten" party the impression that they knew all was finished for them and moved around cautiously in groups.

Type of country:

As in Bohemia, the Moravia villages have only a few kilometres between them and in many parts the villages are very spread out with houses and farms dotted about all over the countryside. This fact led to much of the difficulty in choosing suitable D.P.s where men and stores could be safely dropped away from villages. In this country a successful drop where the operation was not detected was unique.

On many occasions [Redacted] were obliged to seek lodgings at random with members of the organisation and were always given every help. Early in 1945 three groups of Russian partisans were working. They were formed by six Russian-Czech parachutists dropped into the Protectorate from the East. These men were usually in Czech-Russian Forces. They recruited escaped Russian prisoners. Czech civilians gave the parachutists from the East and West the same help and loyalty.

Political feeling: The Council of Three was essentially non-political but when Russian planes began dropping supplies from the East there was a big swing in that direction.

[Redacted] had a very hard job in the Field to keep up British prestige, and reported these developments to London.

On several occasions fights broke out between members of the organisation over the intentions of England and the – at that time – active operations from Russia. [Redacted] had come to promise the supply of arms from the West and was most bitter in the failure to supply.

[Redacted] had unlimited manpower at his disposal with which to form his reception committees.

Lesy potential strength: At D.P. Lesy where he waited for his special equipment and arms, he had 60 people standing by on each of the four times the operation was attempted from Italy. [Redacted] had himself arranged 4 D.P.s each with 60 people standing by to receive arms and states that had his parties received successful sorties to these points he could have trebled the number.

The greatest danger to agents in the field were German Schutzpolitzei.

The Council of Three remained permanently in hiding but most other members of the organisation moved around in the open. There was little or no fraternisation, except for open collaborators between Germans and Czechs.

German strength: Until the last weeks of the war German strength was not very great in this area, and the Germans were afraid to tackle large reception parties.

Sabotage: At Novo Mesto [Redacted] organised the destruction of a railway line at two points.

Summing up

[Redacted] was of the most highly trained agents despatched to Czechoslovakia.

The fact that the "Tungsten" operation achieved little was certainly not his or [Redacted]'s fault. They were victims of high policy and circumstances. Higher policy had decided that the organisation in Czechoslovakia would not be armed to an extent sufficient to start a rising, whereas the report and also others from the Field clearly indicated that had the arms been delivered early enough and in large quantities it is possible that the great underground organisation in Moravia would have completely paralysed the German lines and communications in the path of the Russian advance – if they had not been able completely to liberate their own country.

[Redacted] knew this situation and saw it clearly. He made impassioned appeals to London for help. Although he was essentially pro-British it was easy to see that his feelings for the West were bordering on hatred when supplies often promised failed to arrive and he was repeatedly expected to explain this away to the Czechoslovakia underground organisations.

Against this, [Redacted] has been assured that in the last month of the war desperate efforts were made by the R.A.F. and American fliers to supply him, four operations being flown to the Lesy D.P. alone, all of which failed.

Investigation of the causes of these failures have led only to confusion and contradiction, and after long and searching enquiry from the two opposite sources, viz the boys on the ground and the R.A.F., the only thing that one can be certain of is that each thinks the other at fault. Nevertheless, the presence of the "Tungsten" party in Moravia was a great stimulus to existing organisations waiting for instruction in underground activity and sabotage.

Chapter 17

"Platinum"

Names and Rank:	Captain Nechansky S/M Vynahk, W/T Op. S/M Pesan Sergeant Klemes, W/T Op.
Mission:	To organise reception of stores and agents and eventually to prepare landing grounds for the reception of planes. For reception of aircraft Nechansky had been specially trained in England.
Date dropped	16 February 1945.
D.P. location:	D.P. was near Nasavrky in eastern Bohemia. This was the intended dropping point.
W/T equipment	Two A.P.5, two Eurekas, two R.B.Z.s, one O.P.3, one hand charger, W/T spares etc.
First contact	First contact with London was made on 25 February 1945.
Details of drop:	All men jumped with X type parachutes. No containers were dropped. Vynahk and Klemes jumped with leg bags, Nechansky and Pesan with chest bags. This was because leg bags were not available for the whole party at the Italian base in September 1944. At that time it was arranged for Nechansky and Pesan to attend the parachute school at Brindisi in southern Italy. On their return from this course

both of them stated emphatically their preference for this type of jumping equipment.

Weather: On the night of their operation the weather was good, a clear starry night, but no moon. Snow lay on the ground and the light was good.

The flying operation was carried out by a Polish crew in a Halifax aircraft. The aircraft approached the target and made three runs to drop the men. On the first run Nechansky and Klemes were dropped. On the second run the aircraft was very much off course, failing to see the light from Nechansky's torch. On the third run Vynahk and Pesan dropped to the original point, now indicated by the torches of the previous jumpers.

On this flight the navigator, by pre-arrangement, took a Eureka beacon from the "Tungsten" party. However, to the actual D.P., the party dropped blind.

Height: Each man fixed his own bag. Vynahk and Klemes with the aid of a despatcher. When Nechansky jumped he released his chest bag easily since it was of a simple construction and consisted of an ordinary rucksack with ropes to go over the shoulders. Pesan jumped also with chest bag. All men jumped from 1,500 feet.

Leg bags: The two chest bags were not fitted with friction grips but Nechansky let out his cord slowly hand by hand, and dropped onto a frozen field, without injury, chest bags and contents were o.k. Nechansky was carrying in his chest bag Eureka, carbines, ammunition and personal equipment.

Casualties: As Klemes dropped he lost his leg bag at 250 feet, the suspension rope snapped and the leg bag fell away from him. Nechansky heard the bag hit the ground 100 yards away.

Apart from this Klemes' jump was comfortable. In his leg bag Klemes was carrying W/T equipment, R.B.Z.s, and spares, all of which were destroyed.

After dropping, Nechansky and Klemes flashed their torches to the plane enabling Vynahk and Pesan to drop immediately overhead. Vynahk also lost his leg bag at 150 feet. His bag was equipped with a friction grip, but after a few seconds he saw the end of the suspension rope going through the friction grip leaving a few yards of rope attached to the harness. This case of rope snapping is identical to that of Klemes. Nechansky confirms that on the day of the operation all cords were checked by him and each man personally.

Pesan's chest bag fell away from him immediately his parachute opened. He failed to produce a reason for this casualty. In his bag he was carrying one Eureka and personal kit, all of which was destroyed. Pesan believes that the bag fell from his shoulder when, after falling through the hole he was "knocked for six" by the slip stream.

Bag weights: His bag weighed 70 lbs. Nechansky's, Kleme's and Vynahk's bags also weighed 70 lbs.

Of the whole "Platinum" party, only Nechansky's bag dropped without damage to the contents, namely one Eureka. Nechansky confirms that Pesan's cord was insecurely tied to his harness, but in the case of Vynahk and Klemes the cords definitely snapped. All four dropped within 150 yards of each other.

Nechansky pays tribute to the splendid job done by the Polish crew.

W/T measures: After the drop Nechansky managed to fix up and repair one transmitter AP.5. He did this by taking the remaining undamaged parts of the two AP.5s and putting them together, and as previously reported, on this emergency set made first contact with London on the 25 February 1945.

On this set they were able to transmit, but not receive, and in the first message to London asked London to acknowledge receipt of the message by broadcast of a slogan over the Czech B.B.C. news. This they heard in the field.

London contact: By this means arrangements were made for a relief operation to supply new W/T equipment, and on 22 March 1944, two B.2s and one Simandl were dropped successfully to them in operation "Bauxite 1", which included dropping of Captain Hromak. In this operation Hromak and all equipment dropped without damage.

Split up of party: After this operation the "Platinum" party split up into two, Nechansky and Klemes taking one B.2, Vynahk and Pesan taking the other equipment.

W/T performance: Throughout all W/T contacts the B.2s were excellent and gave no trouble. Nechansky sent his Simandl to the "Calcium" S.I.S. party.

On the maintenance of W/T equipment, Vynahk did most of the work. In all the reception operations Eurekas worked perfectly. Signal plans were carried by Vynahk and Klemes on their persons, working with two signal plans to London and one to Italy.

Documents:	Documents were checked and came through without trouble. Klemes was once in difficulties at Brno where all people had to report to the Gestapo to have their books marked with a red stamp. Eventually "Platinum" party got hold of one of these and helped themselves.
Experiences after drop:	After the whole party had touched ground, the boys soon got together, and after collecting and hiding all their equipment, they spread out to look for Pesan's chest bag which was not found.

A month later they heard that it had been conveniently found by a member of the organisation. At the dropping point there was not a soul to be seen, their drop being unobserved by the neighbouring villages. Their parachutes they hid under mountains of snow in thick forests, where they heard they were found a few days later by a civilian and handed over to the Gendarmerie.

In this part of the country the Czech gendarmerie was mixed with a German Schutspolitzei. Carrying their equipment and taking a compass bearing with their maps they started to walk in a south-easterly direction towards their first safe address. None of them were familiar with the district, but after walking one hour and a half they emerged from the woods to see a signpost on the road with all the directions they required. |
| First address: | At the first address the house owner apparently had not listened to the broadcast slogan from London warning the Field of "Platinum's" arrival. This was now approximately 04.00 hours, and sticking his head out through the bedroom window the house holder said that he would not |

open the door as he did not trust them. Nechansky asked him his name, but the reply was not forthcoming. This man was given to Nechansky as a safe contact from the organisation in the field in London, but at this critical moment he funked his responsibility.

The boys then decided to look for their second address quickly as dawn was one hour away. However, on second thoughts they decided to spend the day in the woods and contact their second address that night.

Gestapo search: By this time search was being made for them in the woods by about 150 Schutzpolitzei, who, although remarkably close to them, missed them. After dark the boys set out for the second address. Here lived a woman and her daughter, neither of whom knew the password. The man of the house, the intended contact, had fled from the Gestapo and was living illegally, and he had left the house ten days before.

Up to one hour before the "Platinum" party arrived at this house, two Gestapo men had been living at this house waiting for the husband to return. From the ensuing conversation Nechansky soon concluded that this was the case, but the old lady did not trust them and begged them to leave. Eventually Nechansky decided that they were in safe hands, and decided to come out with his story, and told the old lady that they were parachutists and had come to contact her husband. Still they were regarded with suspicion but when Nechansky presented the old lady with two large two pound bars of milk chocolate she was convinced.

The old lady then revealed that she was a member of the branch organisation and sent word immediately to the local leader at Nasavrky, from where word was sent to Colonel Steiner, one of the main organisation leaders. Steiner immediately sent three men to fetch the "Platinum" party. After picking up their equipment they all set out at night and walked 23 miles through Moravia to Velkemerzerice.

London contact "Calcium": After a few days rest at Novemesto they contacted Steiner and arranged for emergency messages to be sent through to London by S.I.S. party "Calcium", asking for their emergency W/T stores operation.

In the meantime, Nechansky contacted the whole of the organisation in the "Calcium" group and instructed them in reception work. Later he went to Brno to contact further organisations to find out the potential strength of local reception committees and prepare plans for future operations.

Then at the date fixed for the stores operation he went back to a point between Novemesto and Velkemerzerice. Here he heard the slogan for the operation "Potok", so Nechansky decided to make for this dropping point. "Potok" operation was laid on for [redacted] of the S.I.S. party "Tungston".

Contact: Lack of communication with London was the reason for [redacted] being unable to warn London that he was not prepared for this operation since his Eureka was not working. This operation was to supply him with his new W/T equipment.

"Potok" success: As a result of this, Nechansky set up his Eureka in his own reception area between Novemesto and

Velkemerzerice and prepared to receive "Potok" operation. Homing to Nechansky's Eureka this operation was a complete success.

D.P. confusion: At this time considerable confusion existed between operational base in Italy, headquarters London, and the Field, and in many cases aircraft destined for special operations often turned up at other points. On this occasion the so-called "Tungston" operation turned out to be "Platinum's" own relief operation. Aircraft load was one body, Captain Hromek, four containers for "Platinum" and three containers for Hromek. [redacted] was present.

Hromek: Hromek was in a state of confusion and was nervous, made a nuisance of himself by pulling his pistol on the first people who approached, and according to Nechansky did not know which containers were his property. As a result, members of the reception committee opened up his containers and helped themselves to his chocolate and cigarettes. Later Hromek set off with seven people carrying his equipment.

"Platinum" separation: "Platinum then, with their new equipment, went to the village of Bitec, where Nechansky fixed up operations "Pec", "Okno" and "Kadno". At this stage the party separated and Vynahk arranged operation "Jarro". The parties heard from London the first slogans for these operations on 16 April. That same night Russian planes were dropping stores to Russian partisans.

Brno: In the distance they could see Brno burning during a bombing attack. There were lots of planes in the air, Russian and German.

Lesy stores:	That same night a single plane with all its lights on flew over the area. Nechansky stood by to see what this aircraft would do. The aircraft circled and gave a signal from its Rebecca. This was not a signal that Nechansky knew and it turned out to be the Eureka Rebecca signal for the Lesy operation. In spite of this the pilot dropped his full load consisting of two packages and 16 containers of arms and ammunition. Amongst these containers there were three specially marked Lesy. The drop and the reception were effectively carried out but the Lesy dropping point was 22 kilometres away.
Arms reception:	All the containers and packages in carts and lorries were taken away and hidden in the forest. Next day Nechansky went with Eureka to the Kamna dropping point and successfully received sixteen containers, twelve packages of arms and sabotage materials. To get this load away, Nechansky surprised a bus owner in bed and forced him at pistol point to get his bus out.
Nechansky in Prague:	The next day Nechansky met Steiner again who gave him a new briefing and sent him to Prague. The first stage of Nechansky's journey to Prague with Klemes, was with W/T concealed in a horse and cart, Steiner had arranged Prague contacts, and a car came out to Třebič to pick them up.
German controls:	On the road to Prague in the car they were stopped eight times by German controls. At these points the Germans accepted their personal documents, but were very strict about the authority for the use of the car. Klemes had his W/T equipment casually housed in the boot of the car.

National Council:	They arrived in Prague on 26 April and made straight for the Headquarters of the National Council, which at the time was the head of all groups of the Czech underground. "Platinum" W/T was the first set to arrive in Prague, and the National Committee were overjoyed to have Nechansky and his equipment. At once Nechansky set up a W/T station in order to transmit for the National Council and immediate contact was made with London.
Preparation for the rising:	Nechansky toured the city and rounded up all likely people to join the movement of the Prague rising. Up to this moment organisations existed independently, and the time had come for a co-ordination and centralisation of command. All organisations were pathetically short of arms. Some weeks before the rising Nechansky transmitted to London five chosen dropping points intended to receive arms and equipment to support the rising. On 28 April, Nechansky was back in Prague. The majority of the National Committee members were living illegally. The "Platinum" members lived illegally throughout their entire operations in the country. In Prague meetings to organise the rising were held in various offices and buildings in the town.
Prague tension:	By 30 April, the atmosphere in Prague was very tense, and at this time Nechansky was advised by the National Council to make active preparations for the rising.
Requests for arms:	Repeated requests were made to London over the "Platinum" link for arms and ammunition. A reply was received from London to the effect that 24

bombers would supply the necessary equipment. These operations did not materialise. This unfortunate inability to supply Prague people with the equipment aroused the keenest disappointment in the Czechs with the effort from the west.

Rumours raced through the town that the Americans were on the way to Prague, and it was on this belief that the people took things into their own hands and started many anti-German demonstrations which eventually led to street fighting.

First incidents: First they began rubbing out the German names of streets, then they put out their Czech flags. The next step was to disarm the German soldiers.

Nechansky's command: Observing all these developments, and realising that matters would soon reach a chaotic stage unless organised, Nechansky gave all his sub-leaders the word to take posts. In a matter of hours throughout Prague scores of small independent groups were standing by. Barricades were built all over the town, the people tore up roads to build their barricades and behind them they stood by with what few arms they possessed, and in most cases successfully misled the Germans on the strength of their fire power.

Barricades: Without these barricades German tanks would have swept through the town and might even have destroyed it. Later Nechansky was able to get some tanks and replied to the enemy accordingly.

The biggest fighting was in Pankras, Vysočany, and at the top of Vaclaske Namesti. Nechansky's first attack was on the radio station which was taken very quickly. Here a broadcast was made to the people of Prague for help.

	During this time Klemes was transmitting to London, giving them a picture of the Prague situation.
Arrival of Russians:	In the early hours of 8 May the first Russian tanks moved in, but by this time the Germans had capitulated, with the exception of a few remaining S.S. Units.
Casualties:	Casualties in the rising, numbered approximately two thousand people killed and two to three thousand people injured. Nechansky's concluding remark was: Had help arrived from England at the critical time public feeling in Prague and the whole of the country would have been fanatically pro-British.

Vynahk's Story
After division of "Platinum":

After the "Platinum" stores dropped from Italy, from which they were supplied with their main W/T equipment, Vynahk and Pesan were given a separate briefing to form their own independent party. On the night of 15 April, Vynahk and Pesan set out on their own and at the instructions of the Council of Three placed themselves at the disposal of the organisation commander at Velkemerzerice. Vynahk acted as W/T Operator, and established quick contact with London.

Pesan helped him with coding and decoding. Both made quick contacts with the local organisation and gave them instructions in the reception of stores. They lived in a small village, Hrbov, going out only at night. They met with great assistance from all the members of the organisation who showed great enthusiasm for them and asked them countless questions about England.

Operation "Jarro":	With this organisation they successfully received a full load of 16 containers and 12 packages in operation "Jarro". Political tendencies in this area were no more for the east than for the west, and Vynahk reports that the Agrarian parties always helped them in their efforts.
Gestapo, near miss:	Vynahk was then ordered by the Council of Three to report to Captain Brisa in Novemesto, the organisation headquarters. When Vynahk arrived at the house of Brisa and was approaching the front door three Germans appeared from some corner and were closing up on him from a distance of some fifty yards. Vynahk made a quick decision to run for it, at the same time taking out his pistol. As they ran for him Vynahk shot the nearest German, injured another and got away.
W/T equipment:	Of his W/T equipment, Vynahk pays great tribute to his B.2. set, which together with the British Eureka, worked perfectly. Vynahk reported to Prague on 25 May.

Summing Up

With the exception of a bad start when all the equipment, with the exception of one Eureka, was destroyed during the dropping operation on the night of 16 February 1945, the "Platinum" party, under the leadership of Captain Nechansky, achieved outstanding success.

While operating in Moravia the party received four successful stores operations, organised many reception committees, and kept up a consistent flow of intelligence from the Feld to London.

Greatest importance was attached to this party before sending into the Field. It was highly trained and consisted of men of great intelligence and character. It is very much to their credit that after breaking all their equipment on the night of the operation that they quickly pulled themselves together and with an emergency repaired W/T set made a contact with London.

The incidents which led to the destruction of the equipment when it was dropped led to thorough investigation for the reasons of this catastrophe in London, Italy and Prague. As a final word in this Subject of leg bags, it can safely be stated that:

(a) the bags were too heavy
(b) the ropes suspending this weight (70 lbs.) were not capable of holding the bags on a sudden pull.

In the cases of Vynahk and Klemes the ropes were snapped for this reason. Nechansky was the only man of the party who released his bag slowly and by hand. There is no excuse for the Pesan incident which is quite clearly a case of careless preparation when tying suspension cord to his harness. It is believed by members of the party that all ropes should have been tested beforehand to take the shock and pull of a bag weighing 70 lbs.

Although the "Platinum" party was lucky in dropping all within 150 yards, they and the other parties state empathically that all body operations should be dropped in one run only. One of the greatest dangers well proven by our operations in Czechoslovakia is the wide dispersal of the men as they dropped to the ground in two or three runs.

Nechansky on several occasions took risks in the security of his colleagues and himself, but on no occasion did he make mistakes or misjudge a situation. In leadership and disposition this party was ideal in every respect. In Prague Nechansky's activity was outstanding and his training in organisation stood him in great stead when he commanded the underground forces in the Prague rising.

Up till the time when the "Platinum" party divided, Vynahk did a splendid job as the W/T mechanic and it is to his credit that emergency contact was made to London on a set that he had patched up in the Field. Working alone with Pesan he successfully organised the reception of the "Jarro" stores operation.

Chapter 18

Conclusion

The ultimate aim of all S.O.E. work is a general rising of the people in the country concerned which has been planned, supplied by S.O.E. and carried out by S.O.E. trained personnel. While we cannot claim that this theory worked out according to the book, the eventual rising in Prague did show that something had been learned by the Czechoslovaks from us.

The effort may not compare favourably with other more spectacular risings in other countries, but we do feel that some little success has been attained, and that it does in some measure justify the work which has been done.

Summary of Reasons for Only Partial Success in Czechoslovak Operations
1. Direction
S.O.E. never held the reins completely in the direction of Czechoslovak operations. They only really trained, equipped and transported the operators. The supplying and briefing were always controlled by the Czechoslovaks themselves. Furthermore, there was never a separate body within the Czechoslovak H.Q. doing S.O.E. work alone.

2. Inaccessibility of the Protectorate and Met. Conditions
The distance and the weather were always against operations. In the attempts from England the season was short, and weather conditions over the target area at the best of times were changeable.

3. The over-riding claims of Poland
The over-riding claims of the Poles were inevitable a stumbling-block to operations to the Protectorate.

There were few nights when operations were possible, and these nights were generally common to both countries. Apart from this, Polish crews, who manned the aircraft, while never shrinking from attempting an operation over CSR, naturally preferred to go to their own country.

4. Natural hesitancy on the part of C.O.S. to give full directive to the Czechoslovaks

This was due in the first place to the Czechoslovaks inability to give support to their claim that they had a large and well-organised resistance movement. When, in fact, they were able to give figures and locations of their groups, it was too late, as the Russians had arrived on the scene and the C.O.S. regarded the CSR as a Russian commitment and would only allow the supply of arms and materials sufficient to cover the need of the operators we had delivered.

Appendices

Appendice

Appendix A
Situation of S.O.E. Parties in the Field
4 January 1945

"SULPHUR"

1. Name:	"Sulphur", Pavla
2. Members of the Group:	Adolf Horak
	Oldrich Janko
3. Place of W/T set:	Area of Německý Brod
4. Area of their activity:	Bohemia – not specialised
5. Remarks:	There is a great suspicion that they are working under German control. Last communication on 26 September 1944

"CHALK"

1. Name:	"Chalk", Ludmila
2. Members of the Group:	Bohumil Leparik
	Vlad. Hauptvogel
	Josef Kunzl
	Fr. Nedelka
3. Place of W/T set:	Rosice u Cekanic, district Blatná – Eastern Bohemia
4. Area of their activity:	Eastern Bohemia
5. Remarks:	We have not received a satisfactory answer on our security check, we are, therefore, trying to check the reliability of this group through "Calcium"

"CLAY"

1. Name:	"Clay"
2. Members of the Group:	Antonin Bartos
	Jiri Stokman
	Cestmir Sikola, all of them safe and working.
3. Place of W/T set:	Area of Valesske Mezirici.
4. Area of their activity:	Moravia – except the most Northern and Western parts.
5. Remarks:	The group has proved to be very efficient one and totally reliable.

"CARBON"

1. Name:	"Carbon", Jarmila
2. Members of the Group:	Fr. Bogataj
	Josef Vanc – reported missing
	Frant. Kobzik – reported missing
	Jarosalv Sperl
3. Place of W/T set:	Malenovice or Uh. Ostrch
4. Area of their activity:	Southern Moravia
5. Remarks:	We are in contact with this group through "Clay". They have lost a part of the W/T materials; their attempt to establish a W/T communication with us has been unsuccessful so far. They hear our blind transmission and react through "Calcium". Now in daily contact.

"MANGANESE"

1. Name:	"Manganese", Marienka
2. Members of the Group:	Frantisek Biros
	Stefan Kosina
	Drahomir Vanura. All reported missing.
3. Place of W/T set:	Last communication 28 October 1944
4. Area of their activity:	-
5. Remarks:	-

"GLUCINIUM"

1. Name:	"Glucinium"
2. Members of the Group:	Vit. Leparik
	Ludvik Hanina
	Josef Cikan
	Frant. Trpik
3. Place of W/T set:	There has been no communication with this party
4. Area of their activity:	"Barrium" reported that they have lost their W/T matter and W/T operator. Party is probably missing in the area of Tabor
5. Remarks:	According to the last report of "Barrium", Leparik is with "Barrium", no other reports about the members of the group

"WOLFRAM"

1. Name:	"Wolfram"
2. Members of the Group:	Josef Otisk
	Vlad. Reznicek
	Josef Bersky
	Josef Cerhota
	Rober Matula
	Karel Svoboda – reported missing
3. Place of W/T set:	"Calcium" reported that the party has lost W/T materials and W/T operator
4. Area of their activity:	Eastern Moravia
5. Remarks:	Report about "Wolfram" was sent by "Calcium" and by partisans working in that area

Appendix B

Czechoslovak S.O.E. Parties Summary

Name	No. of Sorties	Successful	Aircraft lost	Reason for return	Remarks
Benjamin	2	16/08/1941	-	c, a	Man landed
Percentage	1	8/10/1941	-	a	Party landed
Anthropoid Silver A Silver B	6	28/12/1941	-	c, c, c, b, b, a	Parties landed
Zinc Steel/ Out-Distance	2	27/03/1942	-	c, a	No info of landing Party landed
Steel A Bivouac Bioscope	2	27/04/1942	-	d, a	Nothing known
Canonbury	2	4/05/1942	1 of 6	d, a	Bombing of Skoda
Intransitive Tin	2	29/04/1942	-	c, a	Parties landed safely
Chrome	2	25/05/1942	-	d, a	Packages dropped
Shale	1	29/06/1942	-	a.	Packages dropped
Antimony	2	25/10/1942	-	b, a	Party landed
Sulphur	5	Only from Italy March 1943	-	c, d, c, c, d	No landings from UK
S.I.S. Parties					
Iridium	6	-	1	c, d, d, c, c, -	Disappeared 14/03/43
Bronze	1	-	1	-	Disappeared 14/03/43

a = normal
b = bad weather forecast
c = bad weather on journey
d = bad weather over target area

Appendix C
Summary of Operations

Date	Codename	Bods	Cons	Packs	Eu	W/T	Net Weight	Squadron	Result	Remarks	Conformation From Field
APRIL 1944											
8	Sulphur	2	-	2	1	1)	1,270	1586	S	Flashed safe arrival	All in order
	Chalk	4	-	3	1	1)					
9	Carbon Clay	4	-	3	1	1	1,010	1586	F	Weather	
		3	-	2	-	1	740	1586	F	Weather	
12	Carbon	4	-	3	1	1	1,010	148	S	Flashed safe arrival	
	Clay	3	-	2	-	1	740	148	S		
MAY 1944											
Nil											
JUNE 1944											
9	Manganese	3	2	-	-	1	150	148	S	All W/T kit lost; personnel arrived safely	
JULY 1944											
3	Glucinium	4	-	2	-	2	150	148	S	Party dropped in woods. All kit destroyed Personnel captured with exception of leader	
18	Chalk I	-	-	3	-	1	240	148	F	Weather	
AUGUST 1944											
Nil											
SEPTEMBER 1944											
13	Wolfram	6	-	6 legbag	1	1	360	148	S	W/T Operator captured; remainder ok. Eureka ok	
14	Windproof	4	-	5	-	1	540	148	F)	Aircraft recalled	
	Manganese I	-	12	3	1	1	1,850	148	F)		
18	Windproof	4	-	5	-	1	540	148	S)	Dropped 30 miles off course, but party ok	
	Manganese I	-	12	3	1	1	1,850	148	S)		
OCTOBER 1944											
7	Platinum	4	-	4 legbag	2	2	240	148	F	Cloud	

Date	Codename	Bods	Cons	Packs	Eu	W/T	Net Weight	Squadron	Result	Remarks	Conformation From Field
21	Windproof I	-	15	2	-	-	2,550	148	F	Bad weather – load jettisoned. Containers were medical supplies; packs clothing	
NOVEMBER 1944											
Nil											
DECEMBER 1944											
21	Windproof I	-	8	9	-	-	2,850	301	F	Icing	
	Platinum	4	-	4 legbag	2	2	240	148	F	Cloud and ground mist	
	Carbon I	-	5	-	-	2	1,045	148	F	Cloud and ground mist	
	Wolfram I	-	2	8	-	1	939	148	F	Cloud and ground mist	
27	Windproof I	-	8	15	-	-	3,012	301	S	-	
	Wolfram I	-	2	8	-	1	939	301	F	No reception	
JANUARY 1945											
21	Windproof	-	4	-	-	-	500	-	S	4 jettison tanks containing hand and pedal generators. Daylight fighter sortie	
FEBRUARY 1945											
16	Platinum	4	1	4 legbag	2	3	200	301	S	-	
	Bauxite)	1	-	2	-	2	417	301	F	Weather in target area	
	Tungsten I)	-	12	-	2	2	3,078	301	F	Weather in target area	
	Carbon I	-	5	-	-	2	1,243	301	S		
	Ely 13-1	-	9	3	-	-	2,590	301	F	Navigator fell ill	
	Ely 14-1	-	9	3	-	-	2,590	301	F	Weather in target area	
	Ely 14-5	-	9	3	-	-	2,590	301	F	Weather in target area	
	Ely 14-9	-	12	5	-	-	3,460	301	F	Weather in target area	
	Ely 16-1	1	12	5	-	-	3,460	301	F	Weather in target area	
	Ely 16-3	1	12	5	-	-	3,460	301	F	Weather in target area	

Date	Codename	Bods	Cons	Packs	Eu	W/T	Net Weight	Squadron	Result	Remarks	Conformation From Field
17	Bauxite)	1	-	2	-	1	417	301	F	Body with legbag did not drop	
	Tungsten I	-	12	-	2	-	3,078	301	S	-	
	Ely 14-9	-	12	5	-	-	3,640	301	F	No reception	
	Ely 16-1	-	12	5	-	-	3,600	301	F	Cloud over target	
20	Ely 14-1	-	9	3	-	-	2,635	301	F	No reception	
	Ely 16-1	-	12	5	-	-	3,656	301	F	No reception	
	Ely 16-3	-	12	5	-	-	3,656	301	F	No reception	
MARCH 1945											
21	Bauxite)	1	2	1 legbag	1	2	474	148	F	Icing on route	
	Platinum I)	-	5	-	2	1	823	148	F	Icing on route	
	Carbon II	-	5	-	-	2	1,243	148	F	10/10 cloud	
22	Bauxite)	1	2	1 legbag	1	2	474	148	S	-	
	Platinum I)	-	5	-	2	1	823	148	S	-	
	Carbon II	-	5	-	-	2	1,243	148	F	No reception	
	Ely 151	-	12	7	-	-	3,722	148	S	-	
	Ely 155	-	12	7	-	-	3,722	148	S	-	
	Ely 158	-	12	7	-	-	3,722	148	F	No reception	
23	Ely 158	-	12	7	-	-	3,722	148	S	-	
	Ely 160	-	12	7	-	-	3,722	148	F	Engine trouble	
	Ely 201	-	12	7	-	-	3,722	148	F	No reception	
	Ely 203	-	12	7	-	-	3,722	148	F	No reception	
24	Ely 165	-	12	7	-	-	3,722	148	S	-	
	Ely 201	-	12	7	-	-	3,722	148	F	No reception	
	Ely 203	-	12	7	-	-	3,722	148	F	No reception	
31	Ely 24	-	16	8	-	-	4,883	885	F	Weather on route	
	Ely 26	-	16	8	-	-	4,883	885	F	Weather on route	
	Ely 27	-	16	4	-	-	4,883	885	F	Weather on route	

Date	Codename	Bods	Cons	Packs	Eu	W/T	Net Weight	Squadron	Result	Remarks	Conformation From Field
APRIL 1945											
1	Ely 24	–	16	8	–	–	4,883	885	F	Fog and haze on route	
	Ely 27	–	16	4	–	–	4,883	885	F	Haze on route	
	Ely 167	–	16	8	–	–	4,883	859	S	Blind drop. 1 special pack brought back	
	Ely 156	–	16	8	–	–	4,883	859	S	–	
	Ely 157	–	16	8	–	–	4,883	859	F	No reception	
2	Ely 26	–	16	8	–	–	4,883	885	F	Weather over target	
	Ely 27	–	16	4	–	–	4,418	885	F	Cloud over target	
	Ely 157	–	16	8	–	–	4,883	859	F	No reception	
	Ely 169	–	16	4	–	–	4,479	885	F	Fog on route	
4	Ely 24	–	16	4	–	–	4,479	885	F	No reception at 24, 26 or 27	
	Ely 26	–	16	8	–	–	4,883	885	F	10/10 cloud. Engine trouble. Load jettisoned	
	Ely 27	–	16	4	–	–	4,418	885	F	Mechanical trouble	
	Ely 151	–	16	8	–	–	4,848	859	F	Weather over target	
	Ely 157	–	16	8	–	–	4,883	859	F	No reception seen. Haze	
	Ely 159	–	16	8	–	–	4,848	859	F	No reception seen. Weather poor	
	Ely 160	–	16	8	–	–	4,848	859	F	Cloud over target	
5	Ely 157	–	16	8	–	–	4,883	859	F	Too early over target	
	Ely 215	–	16	4	–	–	4,418	885	F	Weather over target	
	Ely 151	–	16	8	–	–	4,848	859	F	No reception 151 or 159	
	Ely 159	–	16	8	–	–	4,883	859	F	No reception 158 or 159	
	Ely 169	–	16	8	–	–	4,883	885	F	No reception 169 0r 164 – too early	
	Carbon II	–	16	8	–	2	4,646	859	F	Mechanical trouble	
	Spelta I	–	16	8	–	1	4,660	885	F	10/10 cloud over target	
	Lesy I	–	16	8	3	–	4,646	885	F	9/10 cloud over target	

Date	Codename	Bods	Cons	Packs	Eu	W/T	Net Weight	Squadron	Result	Remarks	Conformation From Field
8	Lesy I	-	16	8	-	-	4,646	885	F	No reception	
	Carbon II	-	16	8	-	2	4,646	859	S	-	
	Spelta I	-	16	4	-	1	4,200	885	S	-	
	Ely 157	-	16	5	-	-	4,538	885	F	No reception 157, 156, 153 or 164	
	Ely 202	-	16	8	-	-	4,901	885	F	No reception 202 or 170	
	Ely 163	-	16	8	-	-	4,901	859	F	No reception	
	Ely 170	-	16	8	-	-	4,901	859	F	170 and 203 identified, but no lights	
	Ely 203	-	16	8	-	-	4,901	859	F	Engine trouble	
	Ely 158	-	16	8	-	-	4,901	859	F	158 identified, but no lights	
	Ely 159	-	16	8	-	-	4,848	885	F	Engine trouble	
	Ely 169	-	16	8	-	-	4,883	885	S	Code letter not identified	
	Ely 164	-	16	8	-	-	4,901	885	S	Dropped on 156	
	Ely 162	-	16	8	-	-	4,848	885	F	No reception on 162, 169, 164 or 163	
	Ely 153	-	16	4	-	-	4,479	885	F	No reception	
	Ely 215	-	16	8	-	2	4,514	859	S	-	
11	Lesy	-	16	8	3	-	4,763	885	F	8/10 undercast. No reception	
	Ely 157	-	16	8	-	-	4,901	859	F	5/10 cloud – haze. No reception seen	
	Ely 169	-	16	8	-	-	4,901	859	F	Haze on route	
16	Lesy	-	16	8	3	-	4,763	859	S	-	
	Ely 3	-	16	8	1	1	4,718	859	S	-	
	Ely 4	-	16	8	-	-	4,763	?	F	No reception. Aircraft missing	
	Ely 5	-	16	8	-	-	4,798	859	F	-	
	Ely 13-1	-	16	8	-	-	4,849	859	S	-	
17	Spelta I	-	16	4	-	-	4,400	885	F	No reception	
	Ely 5	-	16	8	-	-	4,798	859	S	-	

Date	Codename	Bods	Cons	Packs	Eu	W/T	Net Weight	Squadron	Result	Remarks	Conformation From Field
20	Pugotite	4	5	9	1	2	1,673	885	F	No reception	
	Bauxite	-	9	-	-	-	2,289	885	F	No reception	
	Ely 13-1	(1)	-	16	4	-	4,496	885	F	8/10 over target	
	Ely 13-1 (2)	-	16	8	-	-	5,186	885	F	Mechanical trouble	
	Ely 3	-	16	4	1	1	4,505	885	F	Mechanical trouble	
	Pole	-	16	4	-	-	4,228	885	F	No reception	
	Lesy II	-	16	8	1	-	4,864	889	F	No reception found	
24	Pole	-	16	4	-	-	4,228	885	F	Bad weather on route	
	Lesy	-	16	8	1	-	4,864	859	F	No reception	
	Ely 3	-	16	4	1	1	4,505	885	F	No reception	
	Ely 13-1	-	16	8	-	-	4,965	859	S	-	
25	Pole	-	16	4	-	-	4,228	885	F	No reception	
	Ely 13-1	-	16	8	-	-	4,965	859	F	No reception	
	Spelta	-	16	8	-	-	4,995	859	S	-	

Appendix D

Stores Expended on Czech Operations in 1944

	Sulphur	Chalk	Carbon	Clay	Manganese	Glucinium	Wolfram
	8 April	8 April	12 April	12 April	9 June	3 July	13 September
LMG							
SMC							
Rifles							
Pistols							
PIAT							
PIAT bombs							
SAA							
Grenade, No.36							
Grenade, No.82							
PHE 1lb							
Dem Acc							
W/T sets	1	1	1	1	1	2	1
Radio receivers							
Eureka sets	1	1	1	1			1
W/T stores, lbs							
Binoculars							
Comforts, lbs							
Rations, lbs							

	Manganese*	Windproof	Windproof**	Windproof
	18 September	18 September	21 October	27 December
LMG			4	4
SMC			27	27
Rifles				
Pistols				
PIAT			1	1
PIAT bombs			16	16
SAA			15,000	15,000
Grenade, No.36			108	108
Grenade, No.82				
PHE 1lb				
Dem Acc				
W/T sets	1	1		10
Radio receivers			1	1
Eureka sets				6
W/T stores, lbs			500	500
Binoculars				
Comforts, lbs			317	317
Rations, lbs			105	105

* Also 2 containers of vaccines and 10 containers of field dressings
** Jettisoned 15 containers of medical supplies and 2 packages of clothing

Appendix E

Stores Expended on Czech Operations in 1945

	Windproof	Platinum	Carbon	Bauxite*	Tungsten I	Bauxite	Platinum
	21 January	16 February	16 February	17 February	17 February	22 March	22 March
LMG							
SMC			18		43		1
Rifles			10				
Pistols							
Silent Stens							
Welrods							
SAA			7,500		9,500		300
Grenade, No.36					216		
Grenade, No.82							
PHE (lbs)			240				
Dem Acc			75				
W/T sets		3	2	1	1	2	1
Radio receivers						1	8
Eureka sets		2			2	1	2
W/T stores, lbs	200		75			470	530
Binoculars							
Comforts, lbs							
Rations, lbs							100

	Ely 151	Ely 155	Ely 158	Ely 165	Ely 167	Ely 156	Ely 26**
	22 March	22 March	23 March	24 March	1 April	1 April	4 April
LMG	4	4	4	4	4	4	4
SMC	29	29	29	24	54	54	54
Rifles	30	30	30	30	30	30	30
Pistols							
Silent Stens							
Welrods							
SAA	26,340	26,340	26,340	25,050	37,496	39,800	37,496
Grenade, No.36	108	108	108	108	108	108	108
Grenade, No.82	80	80	80	160	240	240	240
PHE (lbs)	480	480	480	240	500	500	500
Dem Acc	143	143	143	143	143	143	143
W/T sets							
Radio receivers							
Eureka sets							
W/T stores, lbs							
Binoculars	5	5	5	5		5	
Comforts, lbs							
Rations, lbs							

	Carbon II	Spelta I	Ely 169	Ely 164	Ely 215	Lesy	Ely 3
	8 April	8 April	8 April	8 April	8 April	16 April	16 April
LMG	2	4	4	4	2	4	4
SMC	27	36	54	36	45	27	36
Rifles	8	24	30	30	40	8	30
Pistols	45	45		45		45	45
Silent Stens							
Welrods							
SAA	33,077	27,525	36,800	42,925	37,052	35,325	39,225
Grenade, No.36	108	108	108	108	108	48	48
Grenade, No.82	240	240	240	240	240	240	240
PHE (lbs)	480	480	500	480	500	240	240
Dem Acc	90	90	143	143	143	143	143
W/T sets	2	1			2		1
Radio receivers						3	
Eureka sets						3	1
W/T stores, lbs	400				100		450
Binoculars	5	5	5	5	5	5	5
Comforts, lbs							
Rations, lbs						250	

	Ely 13-1	Ely 4***	Ely 5	Ely 13-1	Spelta II
	16 April	16 April	17 April	24 April	25 April
LMG	4	4	4	4	4
SMC	45	45	36	36	36
Rifles	30	30	30	30	30
Pistols	44	45	45	45	45
Silent Stens		9	9		
Welrods			10		
SAA	41,825	41,285	42,285	38,925	44,925
Grenade, No.36	48	48	48	84	84
Grenade, No.82	240	240	240	240	240
PHE (lbs)	440	240	240	480	480
Dem Acc	143	143	143	143	143
W/T sets					
Radio receivers					
Eureka sets					
W/T stores, lbs	400				
Binoculars	5	5	5	5	5
Comforts, lbs		120	120		
Rations, lbs		135	125		

* Jettisoned
** Load jettisoned
*** Load lost

Appendix F

The Slovak Rising

Report on a Discussion with General Golian at Tri Duby, Slovakia
7 October 1944

1. Through the friendly co-operation of the Central European Sector of S.B.S. (O.S.S.) and the 15th Army Air Force I flew on October 7th from Bari to Tri Duby, in Slovakia, in one of a flight of six Fortresses, which were going with the primary object of bringing back stranded American airmen, but which took the opportunity to take in some much needed supplies to the Slovak forces.

    We left Bari at 1010 hours, picked up a fighter escort over the Jugoslav coast, and arrived at our target about 1355 hours. I was accompanied by Lt. Col. Souhrada who had come out from the Czech Army Headquarters in London in order to go to General Golian's Headquarters in Slovakia.

    As the Fortresses flew with less than their normal crew owing to the weight of stores and the number of passengers they were carrying, Lt. Col. Souhrada and I each manned a waist gun on the way out. Fortunately, we had no need to use them, and the flight in both directions was in fact uneventful except that the aircraft we were in got bogged in a soft spot on the airfield while taxi-ing round after landing, and could not leave with the others. I therefore came back in another.

2. The airfield lies in a basin in the hills, and is only approachable from North or South. It has no metalled runway, but except for the soft spot in which our aircraft was caught, the surface is quite good grass and the other aircraft had no difficulty either in landing or in taking off. The fighter escort did not land but cavorted about above the airfield until we took off again.

Warning had of course been given by radio of our arrival, and the unloading arrangements were excellent. A team of men was detailed to each aircraft to form a human chain, and within a few seconds of landing the load was being handed out. We stayed on the ground only about half an hour in all. Our arrival and departure were watched by a motley crowd of Slovaks, Russians, British and Americans.

3. General Golian was waiting on the airfield to meet me, and expressed the warmest pleasure at the arrival of a British officer on Czechoslovak soil. I introduced Lt. Col. Souhrada to him, and met the two Slovak political delegates and the Slovak officer whom I was to bring back.

After that I immediately went into conference with General Golian, and asked him about the strength of his forces. He described his strength as consisting of 20 Battalions of Infantry, 22 Troops of Artillery armed with 80 mm guns, and with 10 and 7 cm mountain guns. In addition, he had just received a Battalion of 700 Czechs from Russia who were the first instalment of the promised Brigade, and he also had 24 fighter aircraft from Russia, manned by Czechs. I gathered however that as these had been sent without the proper oil and petrol, they were not a great deal of use.

In addition, he told me that he has 15,000 men without any arms at all and stressed how badly supplies were needed.

4. I then asked the General for a description of his present situation, and he gave me this in detail on a map which he marked for me to bring away. He said that his position is difficult, as the Germans are making a strong concentric attack from the West, particularly from the directions of Kremnica and Svätý Kríž Na Hron, while another column is threatening a valley leading into the mountains north of Banská Bystrica, where the Headquarters of the Slovak revolt are situated.

The Germans have penetrated to very near Zvolen, and this thrust is extremely dangerous as it would give them command to the entrance to the valley in which lie the Tri Duby airfield and Banská Bystrica itself. In the North the Germans now command the valley of the river Vah although the Slovaks have a force in the hills south of the road and railway running along this valley.

This force is situated 10 or 15 miles southeast of Liptovský Svätý Mikuláš, astride the road leading southwards into the mountains. Germans have about 4 divisions in all engaged in the fighting against the Slovaks and have Divisional Headquarters at Poprad and Spišská Nová Ves, where there is also an aerodrome, a barracks and a railway junction.

5. It should be explained that the country in which the fighting is taking place is mountainous and extremely broken. Many of the hills are between 3000 and 4000 feet high, and their slopes are often steep. The valleys between them are narrow.

The hills are covered with thick woods quite impenetrable to wheeled traffic and difficult enough for men on foot. The lower slopes of the hills and the valley bottoms have been cleared and are mostly grass. It is along these valleys that the tracks and rare railway lines lead. From the aircraft as we were circling round one gained an admirable conception of the nature of the country, which is obviously suited to guerrilla warfare and disengaging partisan tactics, though I doubt if the mountains are quite wild and inaccessible enough for irregular units to hold out there for good.

6. The main artery of the Slovak territory is now the comparatively broad valley with the river, road and railway line from Banská Bystrica south to Zvolen, in which the Tri Duby airfield lies. General Golian has nearly half his forces, both infantry and artillery, placed in the wooded and mountainous area to the west of this line to counter the German thrust from that direction. The Germans however are perilously near; at the closest point they are only about 10 miles from the airfield, and when the Fortresses had shut off their engines one could on occasions hear the sound of gunfire in the distance.

As I flew over, I could see Slovak soldiers digging trenches only a few miles from the airfield, but I could not see any other signs of fighting nor any devastation. I was told later there had not been a great deal of this, but that four or five villages or small towns had been destroyed. The bulk of the fighting, I gathered, had been fairly mobile.

The Germans have tanks, the Slovaks have none, and have rightly devoted a good deal of their time to attacking German columns in defiles, ambushing German patrols etc. It looks however as though a certain amount of positional warfare is inevitable in the near future if the Slovaks are to hold their main artery.

7. Major Sehmer, the British officer who is at the moment at General Golian's Headquarters, said he thought that the position was very grave and that it might not be possible to hold the Tri Duby airfield for much more than a week. General Golian himself, who makes a cool and calm impression, said he thought that under present circumstances he could hold out for two or three weeks more, although further withdrawals would be necessary. I gather that a reserve airfield is in preparation.

8. I explained to the General that a sort of informal agreement had been made between the British, American and Russian Governments about the supply of the Slovak forces, and that the Russians had undertaken this task. I asked him what the Russians had sent him so far and he gave me the following list:

(i) 24 fighter aircraft manned by Czechs.
(ii) 700 men of a Czech Bde. from Russia who had been brought in by 43 Russian transport aircraft in the course of two nights.
(iii) 600 sub machine guns, 50 light machine guns, 12 heavy machine guns, 200 A/T rifles, 4 AA guns, [and] between 200 and 300 rifles.

9. Apparently more than this had been promised, but had not yet arrived. Although nothing embarrassing was said, it was perfectly obvious that the Slovaks were most dissatisfied with the Russian help, and several remarks were made about "paper deliveries."

I spoke to the officer in charge of Ordnance on General Golian's staff and he said that although the Czech Battalion which had arrived had been well equipped, the other arms sent were some of them in very bad condition. General Golian was very tactful on this point, but his feelings and those of his staff were quite clear.

This confirms a previous report from Major Sehmer in which he said that General Golian was at pains to make clear that he is not under Russian control even though there is a considerable number of Russian officers at his Headquarters and a considerable number of Russian-officered partisan bands in his territory.

10. Although General Golian had been previously warned by Czech Headquarters in London that I was not empowered to promise him supplies or weapons, he stressed his shortage very strongly and begged me to do my best to send him more. He was obviously delighted at the arrival of the six aircraft loads, and in particular with the Bazookas, as the Slovak troops have been at a considerable disadvantage in facing German tanks. He also needs some mortars, but his chief need is small arms for the force of 15,000 men he cannot equip at all at the moment.

Several Russian officers watched our stores being unloaded, and it will be interesting to see whether the Soviet Government protests to the State Department at this intrusion into a Russian sphere of influence. As our conference lasted the whole time the aircraft were on the ground, I was actually the only officer of the expedition with whom the General talked. It was therefore me whom he thanked for the deliveries we brought with us.

My honesty was stronger than my patriotism, however, and I made it clear to him that these stores were of American origin and that the British share in them was limited to a little medical equipment. I told him that I hoped to send him more of this latter in a short time.

11. Another type of help for which the General urgently asked is bombing support. He mentioned as important targets the town of Kremnica, and Svätý Križ Na Hron, together with the German Headquarters, railway and barracks at Poprad and the airfield, barracks and railway sidings at Spišská Nová Ves. But he said that this help must come quickly; in a week it might be too late. I have passed this information to the 15th U.S. Air Force.

12. I explained to General Golian the position of Major Sehmer's mission, saying that its primary purpose was work into Hungary. He understood this, but said he would like to have a British mission with him.

    The Americans are there in some strength and our expedition took in a radio reporter, a cinematograph photographer and others. I do not know the strength of the Russian representation, but there was quite a number of Russian officers on the airfield examining the Fortresses with great interest.

13. In conclusion, one point which struck me strongly was that the General, whether talking German to me direct, or speaking in his own language through an interpreter always used the word "Czechoslovak" in full. I observed this particularly in the very warm welcome speech he made to me on arrival, and it was obvious that he wished to accentuate this.

    It seemed too that he was sincerely moved at the arrival of a British officer, however informally, to discuss his problems with him. The impression with which I left was that he is putting up as stiff a resistance as he can with deplorably short supplies, and I was struck by his clear and dispassionate view of the military situation.

14. Speaking personally, my inclination would be to send him everything one can without respecting too closely the agreement which may have been made that the Russians alone should supply the rising. It seems to me that if for any reason the Russians are not in a position to let the Slovaks have as much as they need, we should step into the breach. The material is being used against the Germans, and I think that is the deciding factor.

15. We took off at 1430 hours and landed at Bari at 1745 hours without incident. The aircraft was lighter in weight by some two tons of stores and lighter in heart by the presence of my three smiling Slovaks and a group of jubilant American airmen who had been stranded in Central Europe for anything up to three months and had not expected to emerge till the end of the war.

Lieutenant-Colonel H.M. Threlfall

Appendix G

The Prague Rising

A History of Events in the Czech Rising, 30 April–9 May 1945

General Situation

During the week 30 April – 5 May 1945, the position in Czechoslovakia came to a head. The first news of trouble arrived on May 1st, when a general strike took place in the Skoda Works, and from then onwards clashes with the Germans were reported all over the Protectorate; on 5 May a General Rising broke out in Prague.

In the meantime, however, on 3 May, Prague had been declared by the Germans a hospital city and German troops had been evacuated. These, however, began to return immediately after the outbreak of the Rising to reinforce the 11,000 S.S. troops already in the city.

Particularly hard fighting broke out in South-West Moravia around Velké Mezeřiči whilst S.S. troops began unbelievable atrocities in Prague itself. Despite all appeals for help none was available as General Patton's army was forced to come to a halt on a line Karlsbad – Pilsen – Budweis, whilst the Russians were still approximately 100 kms. from Prague at the closest point.

During the whole of the ensuing week, therefore, S.O.E. was faced with continuous appeals for help, not only from Prague, but also from the surrounding countryside.

S.O.E. Preparations

On 1 May the following was the position with regard to S.O.E. preparations to help the Czech Resistance Movement.

General Miroslav had approached us with a request to be sent to assist the Patriots, and this was put up to the Chiefs of Staff Secretariat and the Foreign Office Department concerned, both of whom gave their consent on condition that the Czech Government representatives in this country were informed. The latter, however, vetoed the proposal.

There were standing by in this country two Parties:

(1) "Rothman", consisting of 4 Czech operators together with a B.L.O. to be dropped 30 miles West of Prague with a full load of stores, and

(2) "Churchman", consisting of 3 Czech operators and 2 B.L.O.s to be dropped 30 miles East of Prague with a full load of stores.

In Italy there were standing by:

(1) "Foursquare", consisting of 4 Czech operators to go to an area on the South Western Bohemia border, and

(2) "Picotite", consisting of 2 British officers and 2 British W/T operators to go to another pin point in the same area.

Apart from these two Parties, Italy had been furnished with 27 dropping points which were ready and prepared to receive up to a total of 60 planes with full standard loads.

History of Events

During the course of the week 1-6 May, "Churchman" and "Rothman" were prevented from leaving this country owing to bad weather. The same, however, did not apply to all the operations from Italy or from Dijon where the Italian operations were staging, as "Foursquare" was over the target once on May 1st but was not dropped owing to heavy fighting in this area; it was subsequently proved necessary to change the pin point for this operation owing to the pin point being overrun by Patton's troops, and to cancel "Picotite's" pin point. We were fortunate enough to find another pin point for "Foursquare" but before we were able to find one for "Picotite" events overtook us, and the new pin point which we had found for "Foursquare" had again to be cancelled owing to re-occupation by German forces.

No stores were dropped from Italy during this period owing to weather.

Immediately after the General Rising in Prague on Saturday, 5 May, even more urgent appeals for help were received in London through the Czech link, and openly over the Prague radio which had been captured the same day.

On the morning of Sunday, 6 May, therefore, every effort was made to send help not only from this country but from Italy.

A telegram was despatched to "Punch" outlining the situation and urging them to carry out operations if at all possible. In this country the R.A.F. were approached to investigate the possibility of sending supplies (either at night or in daylight with fighter escort), to a pin point which had been received in Prague itself. At first, the idea was well received and a suggestion was made that 24 Halifaxes should be put at our disposal; the requisite number of containers with arms were therefore prepared by us. Further, an urgent telegram was sent to Prague to enquire as to the state of the anti-aircraft defences.

By the afternoon a reply had been received which stated that almost all aerial defences had been removed; however, later in the evening the R.A.F. informed us that they were unable to carry out any operations on the following day; no reason was given.

Meanwhile "Rothman" and "Churchman" were still held up by bad weather.

On receiving this reply from the Air Force, the Chiefs of Staff Secretariat were informed and the political implications stressed. They were asked whether they would bring their influences to bear, as further telegrams of German atrocities were being received. They replied that at this very moment negotiations were being carried out for the over-all surrender of the German forces and, therefore, there was little use for them to intervene at this stage, as no doubt by the next day all fighting would have ceased. This, however, was not the case. During the whole of Monday and Tuesday, 7/8 May fighting continued, and urgent appeals were still received, not only from Prague but also from South-West Moravia where German atrocities were particularly violent.

Nothing, however, could be done as the German surrender was not timed to take place until midnight on Tuesday, 8 May, and it was hoped that at this hour all fighting would cease. Further, by agreement between General Eisenhower and the Russians, General Patton, as already mentioned, was to stand on a line Karlsbad – Pilsen – Budweis, and no operations, including aircraft, were to take place over this line.

On Tuesday a message was received from SHAEF stating that General Jodl, the head of the German Military Surrender Mission, had complained to them that German troops were unable to surrender on account of the Rising, would we, therefore, send a message to the Czech Patriots instructing them to cease fighting the Germans and place all captured broadcasting transmitters in their hands in order that orders to surrender might be transmitted to German soldiers. It was manifestly impossible for S.O.E. to send a message of this nature, and, therefore, the Chiefs of Staff were once more approached in the matter.

They, however, disclaimed any responsibility and stated that as from that morning the initiation of transmission of any messages affecting the nature of resistance in Czechoslovakia had been transferred from the Chiefs of Staff to SHAEF.

SHAEF were, therefore, once more approached with a request for a definite message to send to the Czech Patriots as from General Eisenhower. This they felt unable to do. The day closed therefore with no message having been sent on the above lines to Prague. A message, however, was sent asking them to report urgently on the conditions reigning after midnight on 8 May, as it was understood that if the Germans were still fighting, General Eisenhower would order the 3rd Army to proceed to Prague as the Germans would have broken the Allied Surrender terms that had been agreed between SHAEF and the Russian High Command.

On the morning of Wednesday, 9 May, reports came through that S.S. men were still fighting furiously and in fact were shelling various strategic points in the city. SHAEF, the Chiefs of Staff and the Foreign Office were immediately informed. An hour later, however, Prague informed us that the Russians had already begun to enter the city and accordingly no further action was required by S.O.E.

During the whole of the above period the Foreign Office were kept fully informed of the situation and they seemed anxious from the point of view of political advantage to bring pressure to bear to send help to the Czechs. This, however, in spite of the direct intervention of the Prime Minister with President Truman, was rendered impossible owing to the military commitments already entered into by General Eisenhower with the Russian High Command – firstly because the Third Army was said to have already overrun its communications, and secondly on the grounds of the agreement with the Russians whereby the Third Army would not advance further than the line already mentioned.

Appendix H

RAF and SOE: Central Europe, Supplied by Aircraft Based in the UK and Mediterranean

Throughout the whole war, the main difficulty inherent in operations to Central Europe was the distances involved, and aircraft, whether based in England or the Mediterranean found themselves operating at the extreme limit of their range. This often entailed special modifications to the aircraft, so that they could carry extra petrol tanks.

The shortness of the summer nights made it impossible for flights to be undertaken to Poland or Czechoslovakia during the hours of darkness, and therefore there was a period during the summer when no air operations could be flown to these countries ...

Czechoslovakia

Resistance in Czechoslovakia, although rigorously suppressed by the Germans, began to show itself soon after the enemy occupation of the country. The entry of Russia into the war in 1941 had a strong moral effect on the patriots, and during September 14 major acts of sabotage and a large total of minor activities were carried out. In the autumn agents and W/T sets were dropped, and although weather was bad in January and February operations were later resumed. In an attack by Bomber Command on the Skoda Works at Pilsen, Czech resistants helped to guide the aircraft by lighting fires near the target.

In May 1942 the execution of Heydrich by Czech patriots despatched from this country by S.O.E. resulted in a German reign of terror. Organised cruelty and brutality on such a scale could not fail to be effective, and many Resistance organisations were broken up while others were forced to go to ground.

In March, 1943, the leader and W/T operator of the last remaining S.O.E. party were arrested and committed suicide, but their reserve operator was still able to send messages, and reported that he was in contact with another Resistance group.

In the autumn of 1943, it was decided that air operations to Czechoslovakia should in future be flown from the Mediterranean, and attempts were once more made to rebuild Resistance organisation in the country. The success achieved, however, was small. The distance involved, the almost continuous bad weather, and the difficulties of navigation in Czechoslovakia combined to make S.D. flights to that country particularly difficult. Moreover, the German grip on Czechoslovakia throughout 1943 was still too tight to permit the establishing of subversive groups. A small number of operations were despatched during 1943 and 1944, carrying organisers, W/T operators and a limited quantity of stores to the field.

COS(44)902(O), 14 October 1944

In October 1944 the Foreign Secretary wrote to the Chiefs of Staff, agreeing with the view taken by the C.I.G.S. that large scale air operations to assist a general rising should now be more properly conducted by the Soviet Air Force, and a letter embodying this argument and suggesting that sabotage activity should be continued was sent to General Ingr.

Annex to COS(44), 339th Meeting, Item 9, 16th October 1944

The Slovak rising which later took place was regarded as primarily a Russian responsibility. In January 1945, the Chiefs of Staff authorised A.F.H.Q. to undertake 10 successful operations per month to Czechoslovakia, but bad weather once more prevented the implementation of these plans, and in the January moon period only one daylight stores drop by fighter aircraft was successful. The weather continued poor throughout the spring; in February, 4 out of 15 sorties were successful; in March, 5 out of 14 and in April 13 out of 61.

SOE/45/R.42

A message from the Council of Three of April 1945 sums up the Air force assistance to their country: "We thank you and Allied pilots for the operations. Few weapons were supplied, but nevertheless you have saved many lives, national property, and you have increased Anglo/American prestige. Every weapon will be multiplied many times."